# The Story
of Your Life

# The Story
# of Your Life

## Writing a Spiritual
## Autobiography

Dan Wakefield

BEACON PRESS
Boston

Beacon Press
25 Beacon Street
Boston, Massachusetts 02108-2800

Beacon Press books
are published under the auspices of
the Unitarian Universalist Association of Congregations

97 96 95 94 93 92 91 90     8 7 6 5 4 3 2 1

Text design by Ann Stewart

ISBN 0-8070-2709-X
LCN 90-52593

To "The Class": Polly, Lise, Dennis, Lynn, Kaysie, Maria, Selina, Steve, Judith, Angela, Nancy, and Marcia; and to all the other "students" whose words and work and friendship have inspired and taught "the teacher."

And

to the memory of Christine Scholes, whose life gave spirit to her friends.

# Contents

Acknowledgments · *xi*

Foreword · *xiii*

1   What Is Spiritual Autobiography? · *1*

2   Who Does It? · *10*

3   Why Do It? · *20*

4   How to Do It · *42*

5   First Exercise: Childhood · *53*

6   Second Exercise: Adolescence · *66*

7   Third Exercise: Friend/Mentor/Guide · *77*

8   Fourth Exercise: A Road Map of
    Your Spiritual Journey · *94*

9   Spiritual Autobiographies of a Class · *98*

Appendix · *173*

A Brief Reading List in Spiritual
Autobiography · *177*

# Acknowledgments

I would like to thank the following people, who are among the great number of those whose aid and comfort and advice have enabled me to lead these courses and create this book: the Reverend Carl Scovel of King's Chapel; the Reverend Robert Doss of the Unitarian Church of Wilmington, Delaware; Paul Fishman and Jamie Jaffe of the Boston Center for Adult Education; Mara Carrico and Phyllis Pilgrim of Rancho La Puerta; Ben Yamin Lichtenstein of Interface; Father Thomas Shaw of the Society of Saint John the Evangelist; the Reverend Pamela Barz of the Unitarian Church of Saco, Maine; Sarajane Siegfreid of the University Unitarian Church of Seattle, Washington; Pam Kristan of the Paulist Center of Boston; Sherry Sonnet for word processing and literary care for the right word; Danielle Levi Alvarez for yoga; James Carroll for literary and spiritual insight with neighborhood coffee; Shaun O'Connell for continuing education in American literature as well as twenty-five years of friendship and logistical support; and Wendy Strothman of Beacon Press for ideas, perception, enthusiasm, and making it happen.

# Foreword

This is not only a book about writing your story. It is a book of the stories that were written in some of the workshops and courses in spiritual autobiography I have led around the country in the past few years. They were written by ordinary people, ordinary only in the sense that they are not professional writers. (Some, in fact, have chosen to remain anonymous or have written under an assumed name.) More meaningfully, they are extraordinary people, for they had the courage and ability to go deeply into their own stories and tell them so truly that they seem to be our own. I am grateful to them, and honored to have shared this experience of exploration with them. I did not "teach" them anything, but simply set the stage for their own creation. May the props and pictures and cues I present here serve the same purpose for you, the reader, and your own students, parishioners, colleagues, and friends.

Say you finally invented a new story
of your life. It is not the story of your defeat
or of your impotence and powerlessness
before the large forces of wind and accident.
It is not the sad story of your mother's death
or of your abandoned childhood. It is not,
even, a story that will win you the deep
initial sympathies of the benevolent goddesses
or the care of the generous, but it is a story
that requires of you a large thrust
into the difficult life, a sense of plenitude
entirely your own. Whatever the story is,
it goes as it goes, and there are vicissitudes
in it, gardens that need to be planted,
skills sown, the long hard labors
of prose and enduring love. Deep down
in some long-encumbered self,
it is the story you have been writing
all of your life, where no Calypso holds you
against your own willfulness,
where you can rise
from the bleak island of your old story
and tread your way home.

*The New Story of Your Life*
MICHAEL BLUMENTHAL

The very act of story telling, of arranging memory and invention according to the structure of the narrative, is by definition holy. . . . We tell stories because we can't help it. We tell stories because we love to entertain and hope to edify. We tell stories because they fill the silence death imposes. We tell stories because they save us.

*"The Communion of Sinners"*
JAMES CARROLL

# _1_ _What Is Spiritual Autobiography?_

Each of us could write many different versions of our life story, looking at our experience from a variety of perspectives, all of them valid and "true." We could write a "romantic autobiography," recounting the loves of our lives from that first childhood fantasy (riding into the sunset with the boy or girl at the next desk), through teenage passion (the groping thrill of discovering our bodies), adult commitment to another person and the choice of a shared life. For many people this means marriage, sometimes with children and the fullness and challenge of family life; and all too often comes the wrench of divorce, followed by a slow, rocky process of recovery.

We could each write an "economic autobiography" that traced our handling of money from the first savings account opened with earnings from a paper route or baby-sitting job to the burden of a big mortgage, overextended credit cards, and perhaps a midlife plunge in the stock market. A "physical autobiography" might take us from early dreams of glory on the tennis court or the Little League diamond (a future Martina Navratilova or "Mister October") to later languor at the office, a postgraduate spare tire at the waistline turning into a medicine ball of flesh at thirtysomething, then getting back in shape through aerobics and running and learning one hundred new ways to cook tofu. Other areas of life that could serve as the focus of autobiography include the professional (steps of a career), psychological (insights and growth gained through forms of therapy), educational (the shaping of intellect through schools, courses, teachers).

Stories springing from any of those subjects might form a part of what I call a person's "spiritual autobiography." The physical problem of obesity led a friend of mine to Overeaters Anonymous, where she not only changed the shape of her body (losing more than forty pounds), but of her interior life, when she followed the OA advice to pray every morning and night, preferably on her knees. As a church member she had prayed before, but never on her knees, and that practice, she felt, gave new strength not only to her will but to her faith. Another friend took up the Oriental form of exercise and meditation known as t'ai chi, soon thereafter stopped his habitual use of drugs, and eventually returned to a more liberal form of his family's religious faith which he had rejected as a young man. Experiences like these, beginning with the physical, would certainly be part of one's spiritual story.

You don't have to be a member of a church or a believer in any particular religious faith to write a spiritual autobiography. I don't know or want to create any set of hard and fast rules to define that enterprise, but I found the best clue to what I mean in the *Oxford English Dictionary*'s definition of *spirit:* "I.1. The animating or vital principle in [humans] (and animals); that which gives life to the physical organism, in contrast to its purely material elements; the breath of life."

That definition also brings to mind some lines by Dylan Thomas that express one of my favorite nondenominational concepts of God: "The force that through the green fuse drives the flower / drives my green age." Anyone who feels the awareness of that universal force in their life can write a spiritual autobiography. A person who feels no such awareness but wants to discover it, or to find a meaning in the absence of it, could write about that search: this would also be spiritual autobiography. After thinking of the term as a fitting description of the sort of writing I was helping people produce in workshops and courses, I also learned that it has a rich tradition in literature.

*

As a young man from St. Louis studying at Harvard in 1910, Thomas Stearns Eliot began to express a desire to explore in his work a kind of writing not fashionable at the time, called "spiritual autobiography." I learned from Lyndall Gordon's superb biography, *Eliot's Early Years,* that the poet was fascinated by the process of trying to explain to himself through writing "the sequence that culminates in faith." His own poetry, Gordon points out, elaborates the theme of a man who sees his life as a "religious quest," and his work and life were inseparably part of an unceasing "search for salvation."

Tom Eliot of St. Louis later transformed himself into T. S. Eliot, the quintessential Englishman. This metamorphosis was so successful that we tend to forget he was a midwesterner, from the heartland of America. If Eliot himself tried to forget his New World roots for a while as he took on the accents and manners of an Englishman, he acknowledged his background in later years when he said of his poetry, "in its sources, in its emotional springs, it comes from America."

Perhaps Eliot's impulse to see the whole body of his work as a spiritual autobiography came from America as well, for this was a widely practiced form among the Puritans of New England. In *The Puritan Origins of the American Self,* the scholar Sacvan Bercovitch emphasizes the significance for seventeenth-century Puritanism of "the personal writings of the period, the countless testimonies, declarations, relations, even broadside manifestoes. . . ."

Since many of the Puritan congregations in New England at that time required personal testimony for admission, the writing of spiritual autobiography flourished. Believers and seekers of the period had to practice what they preached or what they heard preached, not just on Sunday but in their daily lives, an effort then called "the art of living to God."

The famous Puritan preacher Cotton Mather was the first American to use the term *biography* in his book on the life of John Winthrop called *Nehemias Americanus* (a comparison of the first Massachusetts governor to the Biblical prophet). This and similar books showing how a man's work fit into God's plan were very popular. If it was possible to write about the life of a famous public figure of one's own time in relation to their faith, it was thus possible to do the same in writing about one's own life. As Bercovitch observes, "It seems well nigh inevitable in retrospect that the genre of Puritan spiritual autobiography should have developed out of the genre of biography."

Both forms, of course, were older than Puritanism or America. No doubt the first humans, sitting around the fires of their caves, told stories relating their life experience to the power and mystery of the universe. It is not surprising that Professor Bercovitch reports "the sudden ascendancy during this period [the seventeenth century] of Augustine's *Confessions* as a model of self-portraiture." *The Confessions of Saint Augustine,* written during the fourth century, was to the spiritual autobiographers of Puritan New England, as it is to us today, a model of the deepest probing of the struggles of soul and flesh. Augustine's work will doubtless remain relevant as long as people try to understand and record the effort to live by a higher power than the self.

In our time, it seemed for a while that such endeavors were doomed to intellectual dismissal. Freud wrote what was perhaps the first funeral oration for God when he put down religion in *The Future of an Illusion.* The devastation of World War II and the hell of the Holocaust led even theologians to proclaim "the death of God" and look for meaning in what Harvey Cox called *The Secular City,* in his theological best seller of the sixties. But Professor Cox, the keenest theological observer of the American scene, observed two decades later in *Religion in the Secular City* that "rather than an age of rampant secularization and religious decline, it [the eighties] appears to be more of an era of religious revival and the return of the sacral."

In an essay titled "And Now, a Word from Our Creator," I reported in *The New York Times Book Review* in 1989 on a number of new novels that reflected "God's presence as an accepted factor in the lives of contemporary people." The renewal of literary interest in what Harvey Cox calls "the sacral" is perhaps best symbolized by a series of lectures called "The Art and Craft of Religious Writing" sponsored by the New York Public Library and published in 1988 in a book called *Spiritual*

*Quests*. The book contains the remarks of its distinguished participants: novelists Mary Gordon, Hugh Nissenson, David Bradley, and Frederic Buechner, poet Alan Ginsberg, and historian Jaroslav Pelikan. Author and editor William Zinnser said in his introduction to the book that "writers whose work is nourished by religious concerns are on a pilgrimage to find the source of their faith as individuals and of their strength as artists."

The pilgrimage to look for the source of one's faith and see one's experience in relation to that search is not limited to artists and writers, but is shared by a growing number of people of many different backgrounds, interests, and ages. Ways of helping people engage in such a quest through writing have been suggested and used by a number of people, including ministers, writers, and psychologists.

One such course was developed by my own minister, the Reverend Carl Scovel, in response to both experiences in his own life and a need and desire he sensed in his congregations. Carl Scovel is a quiet, thoughtful man, skeptical of fads, and opposite in outlook and personality to everything I think of as "trendy." I was not surprised to learn that the seeds of his course in religious autobiography germinated in his mind and experience for at least a decade before he presented it to his parish at King's Chapel in Boston. The other day he told me the story of how it came about.

"I was dissatisfied with the experience I had leading classes for new church members when I was minister of the First Parish in Sudbury [this Unitarian Universalist church was Carl's first parish, which he served from 1956 to 1967]. Part of a ritual that I assume was also practiced in a lot of other churches was for new members to go around in a circle and say Why I am here, or How I came to this church."

What bothered Carl as he listened to people recite such accounts was that they sounded as if they were all telling the same story, one in which the plot always seemed to be something like: "I was unhappy, I left the church, I was rejected, I wandered around, then I found this, and wow, it's terrific!"

There was a kind of truth to those accounts, but Carl began to feel that instead of people using their own deepest experience they were picking up clues about what they thought they should say. "What I wanted to know was what they thought they *shouldn't* say. I thought to myself, I bet that's where the interesting stuff is."

Carl went to a denominational convention in Dallas in 1972 and attended a workshop led by Sam Keen, a writer, teacher, theologian, and workshop leader known for his charisma as well as his intellect. "Sam led us in a couple of exercises that made a deep impression on me," Carl recalled. "One of them is the exercise I use in the course at King's Chapel, where you draw a floor plan of the house you grew up in, then pair up with someone and each person tells the other about his house. It was a real 'opening up' kind of experience for me.

"In the next year or so, I preached a sermon on my own religious development. It was the kind of autobiographical thing I don't usually do, but I felt moved to do it, and you know, people were interested. I think they connected my experience with their own lives. But there was something about preaching that sermon that felt unresolved, and then I thought, why not let them tell *their* stories? That's when I actually began planning the course. I led the first one in 1973, and have offered it every few years since then."

Like Carl Scovel, Bob Doss (the Reverend Robert Doss, minister of the First Unitarian Church in Wilmington, Delaware) was looking for a way to have his parishioners "get real" with each other in talking about their spiritual experience, rather than dealing in formulas and abstractions. This is what he told me:

When I came here twenty-six years ago, I had a background in psychology, and I had done my training at pastoral institutions and worked in state hospitals and at San Quentin. I had used Martin Buber's *I and Thou* to work with groups to begin discussions, and I introduced Buber's work in a talk I gave to a group of psychologists. They thought his work was like their own, in helping people try to "get real," getting groups to level with each other, avoid abstractions like world issues, and talk about what's in their hearts.

I called fifteen people together and asked them to be leaders of such groups within the church after meeting for a year as a pilot group. It wasn't just about religion per se, but about personal development and growth. It was very gratifying to lead it. The next year I launched things with a sermon and asked people to sign up for groups of fifteen. It surprised me how many signed up—we had groups of fifteen all over town, a total of about three hundred people. It went on for four years and then began to sag. Then different kinds of groups began to develop out of those original ones.

I got inspired by the work of some of the new theological writings, like William Hamilton's *Theology as Biography,* Harvey Cox's *Seduction of The Spirit,* and Sam Keen's *Telling Your Story* and *To a Dancing God.* These theologians were not just doing the traditional grand theory kind of thing, they were talking about "sharing your own journey." It's like what the Bible is made of really—writing about our search for meaning is "a way to do theology."

Carl Scovel called me around that time and we began to exchange our experiences in teaching this kind of thing. He was enormously helpful. We both had classes read Augustine's *Confessions* at one point, and compared notes on it. I also used excerpts from contemporary writers, like Katherine Mansfield's journals. I'd been to the Rutgers School of Alcohol Studies, and I had people write a Unitarian Universalist version of the twelve steps of Alcoholics Anonymous. I used Sam Keen's house-drawing exercise, and later tried one where I had people draw a tree of their lives: roots, trunk, dead leaves, branches, springs that nourish it. I also began to have people bring in music that was meaningful to them. I have people bring in some object that is important to them and share it with the group, like a family album, a seashell, a favorite piece of jewelry. One woman brought in her pet raccoon.

My own writing and teaching of spiritual autobiography began with a course I took in 1982 at King's Chapel called "Religious Autobiography." That title is perfectly appropriate in its context. Since a church is by definition a religious institution and its members have affiliated themselves with a particular religion, it makes sense that "Religious Autobiography" be the title of a course the minister teaches to those who wish to gain a greater understanding of their life by writing about it.

When I offered my own version of the course for the first time at the Boston Center for Adult Education, I called it "Spiritual Autobiography" because that term seemed more inclusive. After writing a whole book about my own spiritual journey that came directly out of Reverend Scovel's course, I wanted to give back the gift of such a rich experience by passing it on to others. I thought the most valuable contribution I could make as a layperson and professional writer was to offer the course in a setting where people who did not necessarily belong to any formal religious institution could have the opportunity to look at their life and experience "beyond its purely material elements."

"Journey in Meaning" is the name of the course the Reverend Doss gives at his church in Wilmington, Delaware. I presented a shortened version of some of my spiritual autobiography writing exercises in a course called "The Inner Journey" created and led by yoga teachers Phyllis Pilgrim and Mara Carrico at the health spa Rancho La Puerta in Tecate, Mexico. All these titles reflect a kind of autobiographical writing that comes from the deepest part of oneself, that attempts to see and make sense of one's life and experience in the most complete and meaningful context. Such an endeavor tries to view life not in the separate compartments into which we so often separate our experience, like romantic, economic, professional, physical, mental, or emotional, but as a whole, and in relation to the whole of creation. Perhaps this manner of writing might also appropriately be called "holistic autobiography."

Another sense of this activity is reflected in a definition of religion from the *American College Dictionary* as "the quest for the values of the ideal life." This kind of writing is always a "quest," the kind of exploration T. S. Eliot meant when he wrote in the final stanza of "Little Gidding," the last of *Four Quartets,* that "We shall not cease from exploration / and the end of all our exploring / will be to arrive where we started / and know the place for the first time." In a weekend or eight-session course of drawing, writing, and sharing our spiritual autobiographies it is doubtful that any of us can reach the profound goal Eliot set, but at least we can begin that kind of journey, and, as the old ads for ocean liners to Europe promised, "Getting there is half the fun."

# 2 *Who Does It?*

I am often asked who can or should take the course in spiritual autobiography. Sometimes I am told who should or should not take it or what kind of people would or would not enjoy or benefit from it, almost always by people who themselves have not done it. Based on my own experience, I would say that anyone who has a desire to participate in a course in spiritual autobiography should do it. The only qualifications needed are the ability and willingness to write and share your experience with a group of other people, or at least one other person, and to listen to and learn from the experience of others.

When I say "the ability and willingness to write" I don't mean you have to be a professional writer or student of writing, or even have any kind of training or skill or aptitude as a writer. All you need to have is a story (if you're alive, you have one) and the desire to tell it in words on paper. There is a very small minority of people—even educated and intelligent people—who simply cannot tell their story in any way but by speaking it, and those people of course have difficulty in a process that requires writing it down.

Of the several hundred people in the courses I have led in spiritual autobiography, only three individuals were unable or unwilling to transcribe their story onto paper. Two of those people made some notes and tried to tell their story aloud, but in a group in which everyone else is reading from a paper they have written, that soon gets uncomfortable, and those two people dropped out of their class. Another person did not even attempt to make notes, but talked at such length that I decided I would have to ask him at the break to restrict his comments so others would have enough time. He left at the break, however, and did not return. It was probably obvious to him, as it was to the others, that he was not going to be at ease in a class that required writing things down as well as talking them out. Those were the rare exceptions to the general rule I have found: that anyone who wants to write his or her story (or some aspect of it) can do so in the context of support and stimulation that the course is designed to provide.

When I started to lead these courses in spiritual autobiography, I was surprised to find that the writing done in them by "amateurs" seemed to me of better quality—that is, more entertaining, more clearly expressed, more insightful—than most of the work done in courses I have taught in the writing of fiction and journalism in universities and postgraduate professional schools and conferences. In the past twenty years I have taught at the Iowa Writers Workshop at the University of Iowa, the University of Illinois Journalism School, the Boston University Graduate School of Writing, Emerson College, the University of Massachusetts at Boston, the Bread Loaf Writers Conference at Middlebury, Vermont, as well as at other writers' conferences and seminars throughout the country.

Although those courses were for people who hoped to become—or already thought of themselves as—professional writers, I found most of the writing done there pretentious, mundane, strained, imitative, and dull. In none of those writing schools or conferences did I read a group of papers of such consistently high quality and interesting material as I regularly receive (and have now come to expect) in any of the sessions I have led in spiritual autobiography.

The first time I took the course at King's Chapel, I was impressed and frankly surprised at how fascinating I found each person's autobiography, and I concluded that I simply had the good fortune to be part of an extraordinary group. Each of us felt our class was "special," that luck or karma had simply brought all of us fifteen remarkable folks together into the same unusually wonderful and talented assemblage of human beings. There was a group pride, like people feel when they think they're in the best or most "special" high school, or army unit, or block of their neighborhood.

When I took the course at King's Chapel again a few years later and the same phenomenon occurred, I asked Carl Scovel if this happened all the time, if everyone in these courses wrote marvelous papers that made them feel they were a special group of people. How could all the papers be fascinating, anyway? Weren't there ever any duds? Carl smiled and said "I have never read a dull religious autobiography." Then, being Carl, he paused a moment and said "Well, maybe one."

I reminded Carl of that the other day and asked him why he thought there was such a consistently high quality in the papers produced in this course. He replied:

> These people are writing about what's most important to them, or as close as they can articulate it. When you're talking about the soul, about religious or spiritual experience, you're talking about the center. You're not just writing about "what happened to me," not just "what I did," although that's part of the story. You're talking about that essential dynamic in a person's life that has to do with a major shift in their desire, or their discovery of their real desire for religious or spiritual experience. So you're dealing with that essential and almost invisible motion. It's like the most important moment in a play and you don't actually "see" it—when the protagonist suddenly "sees" or understands or changes, and you never can actually see *that*. You see the result of it when they turn to the door, or faint and fall over, or whatever happens in the action. I think the reason these autobiographies are always so interesting is that they always have to do with that central action. Another way of saying it is that "God is never boring."

The people in this course are in a place where they are

permitted to talk about what's most important, because it's religious, or spiritual, and that's usually not OK to discuss, even in some churches. You can talk about sex and politics, but you're not allowed to talk about that which is most important, so for many people this is the first time they can express what they feel and have experienced in this whole realm (God, religion, soul, spirituality) that's so crucial but is usually taboo to discuss.

Carl's explanation reveals why these autobiographies are so interesting. I think the excellence of the writing also stems from the fact that people in the spiritual autobiography course are simply trying to tell their story as directly and clearly as possible. They are not burdened by any self-conscious regard for literary style, potential market for publication, or grade (none is given). The only consideration is the kind of goal that Emerson urged in his eloquent 1838 "Address" to the Harvard Divinity School, which ought to be emblazoned on the notebook and heart of every person attempting to write anything more than a summation of somebody else's thoughts or work. It is the only standard for people engaged in writing spiritual autobiography: "But speak the truth, and all nature and all spirits help you with unexpected furtherance. Speak the truth, and all things alive or brute are vouchers, and the very roots of the grass underground there, do seem to stir and move to bear you witness."

Too often, that clear aim is deflected or distorted for people in college or professional writing courses when they try to imitate the style of William Faulkner or Saul Bellow or some more recent literary idol, or when they aim for publication in *The New Yorker* or by Random House, or try to win any prize from the Pushcart to the Pulitzer. They often mistakenly strain for some self-conscious effect that confuses pretentiousness with originality, imagines that muddled prose and incomprehensibility are a sign of profundity and depth. (I am reminded of a student in one of my graduate writing classes who read a story that no one else in the class, including me, could understand, and when I gently pointed this out to the author he grinned broadly and said with triumph, "Good—then I have succeeded!")

Part of the reason for the greater clarity and honesty of the work that comes out of the spiritual autobiography classes may also be due to these students' nonjudgmental and supportive attitude, one that is crucial to establish at the outset. At the beginning of any spiritual autobiography course I say something like: "You are not here to criticize your fellow students, but to support them. Listen to their story not for the purpose of telling them how they can improve on it by making it more like you would do it, but to learn how you can better understand your own story by listening to theirs." I tell the group this course will not be like one of those graduate school seminars in which one student reads a story that another pounces on, and then the rest of the class follows the lead like a pack of wolves on the trail of fresh blood. The assurance that this all-too-familiar phenomenon will not take place in our group is usually greeted by laughter and smiles of relief and recognition. Most of us who have taken or taught college or professional writing courses have experienced (perhaps even participated in) that awful ganging-up for the kill on the vulnerable student whose work is deemed unsatisfactory by these particular self-appointed critics. Having warned against this at the outset, I have never seen it happen in any of my sessions in spiritual autobiography.

More women than men usually come to courses in spiritual autobiography, which has prompted some people to speculate that there is something inherent in the process that makes it easier for women or more difficult for men. Such specious generalization has led to the unfounded assumption that "it's a course for women" or "a women's course" or that "men can't do" the kind of personal writing involved. (Fortunately, no one bothered to tell that to Saint Augustine.)

In fact, the ratio of women to men in this course is about the same as the ratio in all adult education courses. At the Boston Center for Adult Education, Executive Director Paul Fishman reports that the overall ratio of students is about 70 percent female to 30 percent male, which includes the whole range of classes offered, from calligraphy to conflict management, winetasting to t'ai chi. According to Fishman, pretty much the same percentages hold at adult education centers throughout the country.

Whatever the cultural or psychological reasons that prevent more men from taking courses in adult education programs, there is nothing about the spiritual autobiography course in particular that is more difficult for male than female participants. Though I hear a lot about men's lack of sensitivity, or fear of revealing their vulnerability, I have not seen that illustrated in spiritual autobiography anymore than I have in other writing courses, where men as well as women write openly and with equal angst about fears and problems concerning everything from sex to coming-of-age traumas.

In a recent spiritual autobiography course one of the most intimate papers was read by a professional man who had to stop twice to compose himself because of the tears of emotion his story brought forth. The other men as well as the women in the group had the same reaction as they listened to his particularly unsparing encounter with issues we all have faced.

At a supper to celebrate the completion of the course, one of the women participants was telling me of an experience of deep and instantaneous sharing she had had with a woman she had recently met, and expressed regretful sympathy that, as a man, I naturally was unable to enjoy that kind of thing with my fellow males. I asked why she imagined that, and she said, "Well, I thought when you men got together, you just sat around and talked about the ball game." I asked if she didn't remember hearing the paper of the man who shared so deeply in our class, and I wondered if she thought him incapable or uninterested in communicating about anything more profound than a sports event. She looked surprised, and said she supposed that was possible. Even though she had heard the man's paper, and even seen his tears, his behavior did not fit her stereotypical image of males.

I know that men in these courses have also had their stereotypes of female behavior challenged and hopefully altered by hearing, for instance, the accounts of women who bear enormous financial and professional as well as family burdens with nearly superhuman fortitude and dignity. I believe both men and women have gained insight and understanding from hearing the "other side" of sexual and marital conflict in the stories of their classmates.

A man I know who has gained insight and healing through work in men's group sharing told me he thought men would be less inhibited in speaking about their most personal sexual experiences with other males, and so could get more out of a spiritual autobiography group in which only men participated. I immediately thought of a paper read in one of my classes by a man in his sixties who recounted his painful sexual initiation with a prostitute while serving in the Army in a foreign country. I could not imagine a more honest and unsparing account of the confusion, shame, and guilt of that experience, which was shared with a group of both women and men to everyone's enlightenment.

I believe strongly that the common sharing by men and women of our deepest experience enlarges the humanity of us all. While I can understand and sympathize with a desire for some groups such as gay men or women to participate in such a class with others of their own persuasion, and it is of course anyone's option to form or join a group of any composition they like, I continue to believe there are great benefits in sharing across lines of gender, sexual preference, religious background, and certainly age.

There may, however, sometimes be a creative rationale for limiting a spiritual autobiography class to a particular group. Robert Doss, for example, has recently conducted courses especially for teenage members of his church. He has added elements designed to appeal more to the imagination and experience of people of that age group, such as asking them to bring to the following session a piece of music they like that corresponds to the mood or feeling of an assigned reading. Teenagers are often particularly responsive to music and it is an important part of their social and emotional lives. "I used a passage from Suzuki [D. T. Suzuki, author of *An Introduction to Zen Buddhism*]," Doss recalled, "and everyone took three or four minutes to give a reaction to it. Then I asked them what it felt like musically, and in response they brought in music the next week that was incredibly on the mark. The whole music aspect really livened it up for them."

Because teenagers share many of the same concerns, this grouping seems to make sense, and Doss feels the three courses he has led with young men and women have been very fruitful, and brought him a much deeper understanding of the problems, hopes, and dreams of the teens of his congregation. "I discovered that young people were more than ever using humor to avoid getting close. There was true despondence, a deep reaction to the meaninglessness brought on by the impact of contemporary society: the threat of nuclear destruction, the ongoing destruction of the environment. Some of the brightest kids were most affected by all this. It was scary."

The use of music could of course enrich spiritual autobiography classes of all age groups, and I think that teenagers can successfully do the course with older people as well as with their own peers, with special benefits to all concerned.

The first time I took the course at King's Chapel, group members' ages ranged from early twenties to late fifties. The youngest participant was a recent Wellesley graduate who was then twenty-two years old. She is now the Reverend Karen McArthur, minister of the Congregational Church of Meriden, New Hampshire, and she told me recently that taking the autobiography course helped clarify her decision to go into the ministry. "I was doing that writing to help me figure out why I really wanted to go to divinity school. I had been confused about what was genuinely 'religious' and what wasn't, and that writing helped me figure it out. I used some of what I wrote when I applied to Harvard the following fall. I wasn't bothered by being the youngest in the class—I thought it was great that there were some people in the grandparent generation, and I got to hear their stories and learn from them."

I have been told that the course in spiritual autobiography was "not for older people," and that they would fail to enjoy it. This assumes that people of advanced age have forgotten their story, or are tired of it, or would be depressed by looking back on it, or have lost the power to desire to tell it. In answer to all such presumptions, I would simply like to offer the eloquent testimony of a dynamic woman on the verge of her seventy-ninth birthday who writes under the pen name "Heleri." She took a workshop I led in Seattle and later sent me the spiritual autobiography she began in the class, continued with a group from that workshop that met later, and finished on her own. This is what she wrote in the last section, called "Where Am I Now?"

"No, I didn't learn everything I need to know in kindergarten. I shall be seventy-nine next month and there is so much about myself I don't know yet. I am still learning about myself, my strengths, how to tap my imagination, my weaknesses that sometimes are strengths too—my impatience, hunger for experience, need to know my body, what it is capable of doing, walk to exhaustion with a pack, explore my fear of heights, test the strength in my knees. I want to see, see everything, all kinds of creatures, birds, how they love and nest, how they teach their young. What I hear. The music. What I can no longer hear. All this. There is little time for it all.

And after that I must learn not only about myself, but about others too—friends, lovers, husbands, children, people with other skills, of other backgrounds, those living in other countries. There is not enough time to do it all. Above all I need to know more about loving.

And then perhaps what I need to know most of all (I had not even felt this as a need until old age): what is the meaning of it all—this life that has spun itself out from a great mass of cotton, wool, and silk, and lies there now hank after hank of thread, while what remains to spin grows smaller and smaller. I need to know what is all this stuff of existence. How tiny can we be, our place in the universe, and still every cell in our body divided into a million replicas of person. What is my relationship to all this? How can I know, through science or intuition—or learn to accept the unknown and unknowable? A life in which we need to know everything, and know practically nothing.

Life is questing. A child dies before me: why? My husband, too. I feel my body grow old. I no longer seek to climb the highest mountain. I swing on the lowest rung of the trapeze. Whisper instead of shout, hum when I once might have sung out. My paintings grow smaller, my dance steps slower, my words more and faster, my thoughts and dreams richer.

I am richer for having read the spiritual autobiography of "Heleri." I am very grateful it was not restricted for reading by people of only the same gender or age group.

# 3  *Why Do It?*

I was sitting at the front of a gym in a health spa in Mexico, asking for volunteers to read impromptu memoirs they had just written during a twenty-minute time period with stubs of pencils in small school notebooks propped on exercise mats. The circumstances were not the most conducive ones for writing, and the whole setting seemed as incongruous for the activity at hand as it was beautifully appropriate for physical exercise. Three of the gym's screened sides opened onto a lovely landscape of trees and mountains that we felt part of and seemed to blend into. Thirty or so men and women sat or lay back relaxed in sweatsuits or shorts and T-shirts, pleasantly tired from a day of intensive exercise that had begun for most with a mountain hike at six-thirty in the morning. It was now past four in the afternoon, and a soft, cool breeze refreshed our bodies, though I wondered how much it could do for our minds and spirits. Was it possible to write anything at all meaningful in "spiritual autobiography" in such circumstances? I searched the room in hopeful desperation and was relieved when a nice-looking man in his forties said he'd be willing to read what he'd just written.

I had asked the people present to write about a person who had been important in the journey of their own lives—a mentor, guide, or friend whose example or influence had affected their development. The man who volunteered read about a high school friend he admired and looked up to, yet also feared. The friend was a natural athlete, a "tough guy" in ways that both awed and intimidated the man who was recalling his influence. As he recounted the elements that made the "tough guy" admired as a teenager, he realized those very kinds of behavior and personality traits were ones that in adult life could lead such a person into considerable difficulty.

As he read the paper, I could sense that in the process of writing the recollection, its author had begun to see his old friend in a new way, to come to a more mature understanding of him, taking an adult view of a teenager's behavior. In doing so, he lost some of his old awe and fear. It seemed obvious that the shedding of that adolescent burden was a relief, a shift in experience that I could feel in an almost palpable way as the man read his piece. The very tone of his voice changed, taking on a sense of quiet confidence as he ended by reading in summation of his old friend: "I wonder where he is now. I bet he's not so tough any more."

There was a general feeling in the assembled group of a lightening, a lifting, as all of us shared with the reader that kind of relief of discovery that changes our perception of our own experience (what I call "re-experiencing") in a way that liberates us. The intimidation this man had felt about his "tough guy" friend for twenty-five years had been removed as he looked back on it from an adult viewpoint, and along with that change came a change in his view of himself. His own inability to be a "tough guy" as a teenager was perhaps not so bad after all, and did not mean (as he had felt in the past) a lack of courage or strength or a failure in his manhood, but might even be taken as a sign of his own early maturity or sensitivity.

I had enjoyed similar experiences of such "re-experiencing" through recollection, writing, and reading to a group in my first class in religious autobiography, and in writing the book, *Returning,* that grew out of it. I had come to see many key people and events from my past in a new light, and this new vision of them seemed to alter the experience itself.

Still, it was not until that afternoon in the gym that I realized something else about this process of remembering, writing, and sharing. As I listened to the story of the "tough guy," I realized that the past isn't just a set of experiences that are irrevocably set, like concrete blocks that can be hauled up out of memory and the unconscious to be reexamined and better understood (in the way that effective therapy can liberate us through greater self-knowledge). What I saw now was that the past can actually change. By remembering and writing down our past from a spiritual perspective (that is, taking into account its meaning in the context of our life's journey) and then reading it aloud to others engaged in the same process, we can sometimes see and understand it in a way that makes it different. Since our past experience only exists now in our own mind—it only "lives" in our recreation of it—our changed experience of it becomes the reality, and in that sense we really do have the power to change our own past.

I don't mean to suggest we could or should do this by *forcing* a past experience to be something different, by denying or rewriting history like a totalitarian government which recreates its nation's past to fit the latest political dogma. I mean rather that our past can naturally change into something "more true" in the re-experiencing of it. The man's adult view of the "tough guy" was in fact more accurate than his teenage perception of his friend.

Thinking about this kind of transformation through writing reminded me of the excitement I felt as an aspiring young author on discovering the potential of personal liberation in the creative act of composing fiction (telling stories) out of one's life experience. I read a book about the history of art that told how the first pictures were made by cave men trying to draw the animals they hoped to kill, in the belief that the more accurate their portrayal of the animal the better their chance of killing it. In a similar way, some Native Americans painted pictures of buffalo before the hunt in the belief that if they portrayed it well enough they would be sure to slay it when they faced it in the field.

This concept of "killing the buffalo" came to represent to me the possibility of destroying my own demons by writing about them as accurately as possible. (This was part of the force behind my first novel, *Going All The Way,* and on some level its writing and publication did indeed seem to liberate me from a few of the demons that plagued my own "coming of age.") What occurred to me in the shift of experience I saw in the "tough guy" story was that one might not have to "kill the buffalo" of past experience, ridding oneself of it altogether, eliminating it from consciousness, but perhaps one could "tame" it—that is, incorporate it into one's whole life experience in a new and less threatening way.

William Faulkner once said, "The past isn't over, it isn't even past." I took that to mean that we—nations, families, and individuals—were still stuck in it, burdened and oppressed by its weight and errors and tragedies. From my layperson's understanding of Freud my sense is that when psychiatry works, the patient is able to "get rid" of the past, or its painful aspects, by bringing it to the surface (the conscious mind).

What I saw as sometimes happening differently in the remembering, writing, and sharing of the spiritual autobiography work was a re-experiencing of the past, not just as it "really" happened, but also as something which can actually be altered. Such a change occurs when we look at the past through the lens of adult experience, write about it from a holistic or spiritual perspective, and come to understand it differently in the process.

From being a writer all my life I knew that much more concentration and focus is required to write something than merely to remember it; that there is almost by necessity an interpretation of material as it is processed from raw recall into written description. What I didn't realize, and would in fact have probably argued was not likely, was that there is a further integration and understanding (and thus alteration) in reading aloud to a group of sympathetic listeners who are also sharing their own experience in a similar way. I learned that from leading workshops in spiritual autobiography.

The monastery on Memorial Drive in Cambridge, Massachusetts is about as far as you can get (on this continent, anyway) from the Rancho La Puerta health spa in Tecate, Mexico. The distance is not only geographical (the tropical southwest to the wintry northeast) and cultural (southern California physical to Cambridge intellectual), but spiritual. I happen to feel both places are very spiritual but could not be more different in their particular manifestations of spirituality. Rancho is not religious in any institutional way, though the mountain called Cuchuma the guests climb every day was sacred to the native Indians, and staff members speak of the "spirit" of the mountain and its surrounding landscape. The Cambridge monastery is part of the Society of Saint John the Evangelist (also known as the Cowley Fathers) an Episcopal order of monks, and is a classic place of worship of institutional religion. The high vaulted ceiling and marble floors of the chapel project an aura of medieval Christianity. Even downstairs, around worktables and folding chairs, one still feels the chapel's awesomeness, grandeur, and tradition above. It is a deeply spiritual place, whose enclosed beauty contrasts with the natural expanse of the mountains seen through the open-sided gym at Rancho.

I was leading a weekend retreat on spiritual autobiography at the monastery with fifteen men and women, including three members of the Cowley Fathers community. In the Saturday afternoon session we did the exercise about a mentor, guide, or friend who had influenced our journey, first drawing a picture of the person, pairing up to exchange "introductions" of our subjects, then writing about how the person influenced us, and finally reading our pieces aloud to the group.

A woman read an account of her uncle coming to visit when she was a child. This uncle was her mother's favorite brother, and her mother was always especially happy when he came. After reading to the group the story of one of those visits, the woman said that in reading it, she realized something she hadn't seen when she wrote the paper. In her writing she described how her mother became much more youthful in the free and happy way she spoke and acted when Uncle Fred came to town. In writing, the author had realized the effect of her uncle's visit on her mother. What she discovered further in reading her piece aloud was that "the way my mother acted when Uncle Fred was there enabled me to see my mother as a different person, as someone who had her own life aside from her role of being my mother, and it gave me a new appreciation and understanding of her to realize that. So Uncle Fred was not just good to me as a kind relative who came to visit and brought a gift. His presence changed my mother, and not only made her happy, but allowed me to see her in this new way, as a person in her own right, who had a whole life outside of me, and that enabled me to think of her as a woman and a friend as well as a mother."

The woman was excited by this discovery, and believed she would not have arrived at it in the writing alone, but only through reading it aloud to the group. I believe—and the students I have talked to about this concur—that the added power and insight that comes from reading aloud arises not simply through the act of speech, but also from the sympathetic audience of fellow seekers engaged with you in the process of discovery. In other words, if one were to read the paper aloud to an empty room, or before a mirror, I doubt that the same kind of additional insight into the experience would be available.

Reverend Scovel affirmed the value of reading aloud based on his own experience in leading the course for sixteen years. He explained that "hearing yourself tell it to other people is entirely different from thinking it to yourself. I got a letter once from a woman I had called on in the hospital who was facing surgery that would end her career. She wrote me later and said 'telling you about it made it real for me, and enabled me to deal with it.' In Alcoholics Anonymous there's a lot of repetition of people telling their story, and it's important in dealing with the problem."

A young man in a twelve-step recovery program observed after doing the spiritual autobiography course that "what I found is I could write something and read it to myself and it would probably have little impact, but if I'm with someone else and read it aloud, there's something about another person's presence that makes it 'ring true.' It's much more powerful."

In spite of the value of reading these personal papers to a group of people, there should never be any coercion to read, and everyone should feel perfectly free to "pass" on any or all opportunities to share in this way. I have been surprised and delighted, however, at the willingness of people to share, even when the group is newly assembled and there seems to have been no time to build a sense of bonding and trust. There is something about the common enterprise itself that seems to create such an atmosphere.

When I gave a workshop at the University Unitarian Church in Seattle, I had only three hours to lead an introductory session on spiritual autobiography. Some of those present were members of the church, and others had read about the workshop in *The Seattle Times* and did not know anyone else in the group of fifteen people who gathered around long worktables formed in a square in a Sunday school room. By the time we had gone around the room for brief introductions, and paired off to share a drawing exercise, there was already a spirit of community in the room, and with each paper that was read aloud that feeling grew.

Jane Smith, a participant who works in an academic office at the University of Washington, explained a great deal about the process when she wrote me later that

> one of the main reasons I found the workshop experience amazing was that I actually had the courage to read my writing to the group, which was a first for me. In fact, it was more than courage. I felt an urgent need to share with everyone in the room. The experience would not have been complete for me if I had not read, and I probably would have felt that I had cheated myself out of something very special. I think that being able to have the option to comfortably decline if I elected not to read relieved me of any pressure and I was able to go for it. . . . I never thought of myself as being able to write (other than business correspondence which I do every day), let alone read my writing aloud to people. Participation in the workshop opened up some valuable windows for me, and I do plan to continue my "spiritual journey" on paper.

Though we had to end the workshop at noon, I suggested that those who wanted to continue writing their spiritual autobiographies could meet as a group of their own to enjoy the support and inspiration provided by the experience of writing and sharing in community. Some of them did that, and several sent me the "completed" or "finished" autobiography they wrote. (I put quotes on those words to indicate the provisional nature of those concepts, since as long as we are alive our spiritual autobiographies are always in progress. We may continue to enjoy and learn from writing them in journals, essays, stories, or any other form, and benefit from reading them to whatever audience of friends and fellow seekers we may find to hear them.)

A member of the Seattle group who sent me some of her subsequent work was Donna Johnson, an artist who wrote on one of the lovely greeting cards she designs that "I hope I'll be writing a lot of things for the catharsis that I don't even need to use in the finished piece, but what I'm sending you seem to be chapters one and nine, if there were to be a ten. I'm even more thrilled getting to know me than I was getting to know you!" She also reflected that "the sharing is so deep in the class. So many of the threads that run through our stories intertwine, it's fascinating how we're all totally different . . . in the same ways."

The first time I led a class in spiritual autobiography I asked the students at the end what the most valuable part of it was for them. The most frequent response was that learning they weren't the only one to go through "the dark side" of a life journey, but that all the others had done so as well, was the most reassuring and meaningful aspect. Each of these people, of different backgrounds, ages, and religious or philosophical beliefs, had written unique "dark side" stories, yet all shared the experience of enduring and emerging from their ordeals, their particular "dark night of the soul."

Of course we also share brighter parts of the life journey that are evoked in the exercises of the spiritual autobiography course—for example, each of us chooses one of many mentors, guides, or friends who has helped us progress along our way to write about and share. That also is important and enriching, but it is a more commonly acknowledged and culturally acceptable experience.

The difficulty and pain of the "dark side" is still a taboo subject, despite all our enlightened "understanding" and admission of the myriad ills and pressures of contemporary society or of the human condition in general. The old American success ethic, so powerfully represented in today's lexicon by the upwardly striving "Yuppie," still makes it a shame to admit failure, be it personal or professional, or to let oneself be seen as anything less than physically fit and psychically sound, a smiling achiever moving ceaselessly onward and upward from the crib to the great condo in the sky.

The competitive strain (in the double sense of that word both as a continuous "streak" running through a pattern, and as pressure) in the success ethic helps divide us into rivals in the marathon of life (what the corporation men of the 1950s labeled the "rat race"). The sharing of experience at the personal level which is part of spiritual autobiography work, on the other hand, brings us closer together, shows us the commonality of our humanity. As a banker wrote at the end of the second course I led at the Boston Center for Adult Education, "The similarities in our lives was a great revelation. The sharing of my experiences and hearing others describe theirs was the highlight of every week."

Even after a brief weekend workshop in spiritual autobiography at Interface ("New England's center for the fitness of mind, body and spirit") in a Boston suburb, participants commented that it had been "a real experience of community," and "truly was community building." As one man put it, "I felt part of a family almost immediately (albeit one of the shy, quiet members)."

Such a sense of community is especially significant in these times, when many of us experience family and community as part of the "brokenness" of our lives. Like so much of life in this speeded-up micro-chip era, the institutions that once seemed solid bases of peoples' daily existence have become increasingly unmoored, not only by divorce, but by the swift change of neighborhoods in the restless movement to and from new (and so quickly old and discarded!) jobs, careers, apartments, houses, condos, cities, parts of the country, and other countries. This seemingly ceaseless flow has made the buying and selling of apartments and houses (optimistically advertised as "homes") one of the principal businesses of the day. As Coolidge once pronounced that "the business of America is business," one might say today that "the reality of America is real estate."

When I moved to the Beacon Hill area of Boston in the late sixties, one of the things I loved about the neighborhood was that it really was a neighborhood, in the old-fashioned sense of the word that meant "community." People on my block on Revere Street knew one another, exchanged greetings and sometimes recipes, shared tomatoes brought from the country, impromptu chili suppers, and punch and cookies at Christmas open house parties. You saw even more neighbors at the Charles Street Fair every fall, and at the pancake breakfast of the Beacon Hill Civic Association every spring. Now it's a different kind of place. A recent article in *The Boston Globe* said that the resident population of Beacon Hill and Back Bay had changed more than 60 percent in the last five years. I recently received an announcement in the mail that there would be no Charles Street Fair again this year (the second year in a row) because there weren't enough people interested in volunteering to do the necessary work and planning to make it happen. The newcomers have no knowledge of or interest in the neighborhood traditions, so the traditions die, and so does the feeling of "neighborhood." It has become just another expensive place to live, with historic architecture.

Like many people, I found a community in church when I joined King's Chapel nearly ten years ago. That sense of community was deepened and enriched when I took the minister's course in religious autobiography, creating a bond with my classmates that went far deeper than the pleasant exchanges at the Sunday coffee hour after the service, or the shared experiences of committee work or retreats. The bond of writing and sharing one's life journey not only strengthened a feeling of comradeship with others in the course, but with other people in general. You discovered you were a part of humanity and realized that the people you saw at the office or passed in the street no doubt had stories that were not that different from your own. Along with that came a fortification and deepening of faith, or whatever each of us may mean by the spiritual element in our lives.

Something like this happens in the spiritual autobiography classes and workshops I lead outside my church, in other religious institutions or in secular adult education programs. The process confirms a growing realization I have had in my own spiritual journey, and a shift in my layperson's groping to understand spirituality. When I first became actively involved in church and the search for spiritual enlightenment, delving into Bible study classes, retreats, and reading religious writers from Saint John of the Cross to Thomas Merton and C. S. Lewis, I developed a romantic idea that "real" spirituality was represented by the lone monk on a mountaintop communing with God in a kind of holy isolation. After nine years of pursuing such matters by reading, prayer, spiritual direction, daily meditation, teaching and writing, serving on the religious education committee and vestry of King's Chapel, going on retreats with church groups and by myself, I have come to the opposite conclusion: that real spirituality comes in community.

In saying this I am fully aware that I speak as a neophyte, and that my experiences as a layperson seeking religious understanding do not qualify me to make theological pronouncements. I offer my thoughts on the subject as the notes of a seeker who started late in life and is reporting findings from his personal experience at this particular interim stage on his journey.

When I say that the deepest and most genuine kind of spirituality is found in community, I do not mean that one must necessarily join a church or synagogue to find it, although many people, myself included, have discovered that affiliation with an ongoing religious tradition and institution is helpful, supportive, and nourishing. To some people it is even crucial. As I wrote of my own experience in returning to church after staying away for more than a quarter of a century, "I was grateful for the sense of shared reverence, of reaching beyond one's flimsy physical presence, while praying with a whole congregation." It was the shared aspect of reverence, the praying with others who were also seeking a higher power that many of us call God, that bolstered my efforts to find a spiritual dimension in my life.

Many people today find their community outside the church, in the fellowship of twelve-step programs like Alcoholics Anonymous that are based on giving oneself over to a higher power, however that may be conceived. I have heard those programs referred to in the past few years as "the hidden church," and I think that's a relevant description. Still others find community and spiritual growth in oriental disciplines like yoga and t'ai chi (both of which have been called forms of "meditation in movement"). Some find their community in service to others in non-church programs that help the homeless, or offer company and comfort to AIDS victims, or reach out to the countless distressed, disabled, and abused human beings of this society.

The connection of community and spirituality becomes clearly evident in the course of spiritual autobiography. Just as people busily involved in church activities find a deeper kind of community and spiritual awareness in this kind of course, so do people without an institutional religious affiliation find such values in the course when they take it at secular adult educational institutions. My most recent class at the Boston Center for Adult Education consisted mostly of people without any church or synagogue affiliation, with a range of religious backgrounds, including two Jews, one Buddhist, two people who described themselves as "recovering Catholics," one practicing Catholic, and a scattering of lapsed Protestants of assorted denominations.

I wondered what effect the course had on the spiritual life of the students who took it in a secular setting, so at the end of the class I asked each of them to answer the following question: "Has this experience affected your feeling of faith, belief, or religious understanding?" Every person felt it had increased that element in their lives, and here is how some of them explained that effect:

> It has not only brought me closer to myself, it has brought me closer together with my classmates. We started out as twelve or thirteen strangers in a room, but we have

come to have a genuine concern and respect for each other that I find very wonderful. I am now more interested in them and less interested in myself than when I started.

————

Being in the group and being able to talk freely about spiritual matters with people who've obviously thought deeply about such things has been an exhilarating and liberating experience. It has made me feel I'm not alone. I have many wonderful, smart, and deep friends and family who manage to lead decent lives without pondering their lack of spirituality. So it's not something I'm comfortable talking to them about and it became easy to push it to the back of my mind. Being in the class helped remind me how important a spiritual life is to me.

————

I am beginning to be more aware of God in other people. And in myself. I also have more questions than ever, which is a sign, I think, of God's presence. I realize now that without questions, I wouldn't be alive and growing. Of course, I wish all this weren't so difficult, but it's all part of the paradox and mystery of God that I have learned to accept.

————

This course is made up of very different people. Unlike a church group or temple congregation, where people have one preconceived religion and program, our group is comprised of people from many religions, professions, and origins. . . . Representatives of a diverse world . . . come together to return to faith individually and unite collectively [as a group sharing experiences].

It is clear that in these assessments by people who took the course, the development of spirituality is directly linked to the community of the class, the process of getting to know and honor the other people's journeys, and to see how much we share with those who may seem quite different from us in age, sex, work, financial status, and religious background.

The appreciation of diversity by the students of the Boston Center class does not mean that the course is any less powerful when done with people of the same church and religious belief. (A student in the course at King's Chapel wrote that "I found listening to other Unitarian Universalist Christians uplifting.") In the sharing of life journeys through spiritual autobiography, people are empowered by the others in their group whether they come from similar or different backgrounds; it is the sharing and honoring of one's own and others' deepest experience that creates the sense of community, and spirituality arises from that.

The power of community in these groups operates in ways I would not have imagined. I had always taken it as a matter of course—more like a matter of pride, in fact—that writing was a lonely business, that it could only be done in splendid isolation, that the writer by definition was a person who stands apart from the crowd, an observer whose mysterious and often painful creative process cannot be understood or shared by his or her fellow humans. The figure emerging from this picture sounds very much like the lone monk on the mountaintop whom I had imagined as the ultimate example of spirituality when I first began to try to understand it. I would have laughed at any suggestion that writing could somehow be aided—if it could be done at all—in a group. Yet that's what happened when I first gave the course in a weekend format at Interface, a local adult education center. There wasn't time to have people go home and write papers alone and return, so I gave them limited time periods to write in class, and then everyone took turns reading. Almost everyone said they felt a kind of group energy that they drew on in writing their papers, especially after the first round was read and the sense of community established.

One man in that class later commented that "the chance to listen to others made my own writing easier, I mean more doable and better." One woman who chose not to read her paper in the first round read a very powerful one at the next opportunity, and said that "the first time I wrote I kept editing myself, crossing things out, trying to hold things back, and also trying to make it sound perfect, so I was left with almost nothing. After I heard what other people read, I felt frustrated that I had held back, and the next time I just decided to let it flow, and I really enjoyed doing it."

There was a remarkable quality to the writing in that workshop, and in other sessions with limited time, when there was no opportunity for people to go home, write alone, and bring back their papers to read later. I found that on-the-spot writing was extremely effective, producing more free-flowing and "open" pieces than might have been possible with time to revise and edit.

The writing in the eight-week courses that provide time to write at home is also of high quality, however, and I am convinced that part of the excellence of these compositions derives from the group energy or spirit of community that is born of the sharing and sense of responsibility to the others in the class. The final eight-to-ten-page spiritual autobiography that is the culmination of the eight-week courses is not an easy assignment, yet I have rarely seen anyone fail to produce a paper of real merit, one of value to the listeners as well as to the author. This motivation was described by a woman who took one of the "long form" courses:

"The most valuable thing about the course was having to get my thoughts down on paper. It was terribly difficult to do the final paper, but flogging myself to do it because I couldn't be the only one to fail to produce and share was good for me, and what I learned about myself was a wonderful outgrowth of the course."

At the end of one eight-week course, I asked the members of the group to comment on whether writing the spiritual autobiography material was easier or more difficult than other kinds of writing they had done. The class was almost evenly divided. Some thought it was more difficult because "it required much more probing, and then tremendous trust to reveal my findings." "I felt as if I were writing from another part of me that hadn't been put into words before; the feelings were deeper and not easily expressed in words." "It was more difficult in that thinking about painful experiences didn't cause me pain, but writing about them did; but it was easier because I found a lot of material inside myself."

Those who found the writing in the course easier said, for instance, "The words flowed more easily, I think because I cared more." "This was probably the easiest writing I have ever done because there was only one way to write my journey. Whatever the assignment was, something called out to be written. I had no choice but to write what was inside." "The writing was easier to begin because of the preparatory exercises and because I was familiar with the events of my life (though not as observant of the details as I might have thought)."

Whether people find the writing easier or more difficult in spiritual autobiography, I am certain that it is richer, deeper, and more rewarding than many other kinds of writing, because of the process of inner exploration it requires. I am also certain that the spiritual aspect (however it may be defined by individual participants) is crucial to the fullness of the enterprise, for it leads people to reflect on their life experience not only in the deepest but also the most holistic kind of way. As one student said of the course, "It made me look at my life as a continuous flow, a pattern of related events, rather than a series of miscellaneous happenings."

This kind of integration of experience through reflection, writing, and sharing from a spiritual viewpoint can obviously bring about effects that in a purely secular sense might be called "therapeutic." The intention of the course, however, is not therapy, which if held as the goal would, I think, distort and detract from the very wholeness of the experience, robbing it of its rightful dignity as a process worthy in itself, and make it instead a means to another end, a cure for assorted neuroses, or a self-improvement gimmick. I prefer to think of any such benefits of the experience as part of a healing process that can arise naturally from exploration and expansion of one's spirituality, in the sense one student expressed in saying the course "has shown me there was a much larger spiritual dimension to my life than I ever would have thought."

The concept of psychological healing as a natural part of spiritual experience has come to be widely recognized in the past five years through the continuing popularity of the best seller *The Road Less Traveled* by M. Scott Peck, a Connecticut psychiatrist. With sales of more than 3.5 million in six years, the book rivals in popularity *The Joy of Sex,* the best seller of the seventies, and indicates a shift in our cultural priorities.

Had a minister, priest, or rabbi written a book saying that

spiritual and religious values and experience can be relevant in healing the psychic wounds of contemporary people, my guess is that the book would have been automatically dismissed. That a practicing east coast psychiatrist wrote it was a cultural validation, and enabled sophisticated, college-educated people to hear and accept its message. That message, summed up in the book's subtitle *A New Psychology of Love, Traditional Values and Spiritual Growth,* has brought about a widespread cultural healing—a healing of what was once a seemingly irreconcilable split between spiritual and psychological values or ways of understanding.

When I graduated from Columbia College and started out in New York in the 1950s, one had to choose between science or religion as a basis for understanding the world and dealing with one's problems. Either you went to church or to a psychiatrist, and very few people I knew did both. Many, like me, substituted psychiatry for church, and felt that the chasm between the two systems of belief they represented was unbridgeable. In my black-and-white view, we enlightened intellectuals stood on the side of science, and a crowd of Holy Roller fundamentalists on the side of religion.

When I was undergoing a rigidly Freudian psychoanalysis in the 1950s, I could not have imagined a psychiatrist writing as Scott Peck does about grace and love in the healing process. Thirty years later, two different people gave me copies of Peck's book for Christmas the year I started going back to church. Reading it was a healing as well as a learning experience. The book's immense and continuing popularity has incited attacks on it which I think are unfair. Critics have tried to dismiss it as another simple-minded self-help guide, and have neglected the thoughtful complexity of a work which promises that "life is difficult" and that "the path to holiness lies through questioning *everything.*"

Through this psychiatrist's insight, we learn that spiritual growth can bring healing that may be also psychologically beneficial or therapeutic. That kind of effect may arise through the work in spiritual autobiography, as many students have reported after taking the eight-week course, weekend workshops, or even day-long or half-day sessions. These are some of the ways they have described such experiences:

I didn't realize how therapeutic it would be to lay my burden down by writing my burden down. Sometimes I look back now and wonder what I would feel if I hadn't. Tragic.

———

I deeply felt some old pains and received some re-markable vision and understanding of them as well as a new hope.

———

The weekend helped me begin to clarify such aspects of my life as co-dependency, my parents' alcoholism, my own self-esteem/lack of it. I don't know if this was intended or not. There do seem to be a lot of twelve-step people and Adult Children of Alcoholics people in this workshop, which I hadn't counted on, so I guess I was in the right place.

———

Having to read papers to others was hard at first, but a wonderful experience—cathartic, really, to talk about some deep feelings and have others validate them by responding sympathetically.

———

I wanted to receive additional understanding about the events in my life, which I instinctively realized could be achieved by writing about them. I also wanted to complete and release the past and my attachment to it for the pur-pose of living the rest of my life with full attention and all the enthusiasm I can bring to it. The course gave me the opportunity to accomplish those things.

———

The general sharing by others in the course encourages one to explore deeper than one might dare on one's own.

———

The course helped me to pull back more layers. And it was such a gentle experience.

It cannot be overemphasized that the "gentle" nature of this process is crucial. The only confrontation in the course should occur between the individual and his or her own experience and reaction to it, never through challenge or critique from the leader or other participants. And in this gentle and supportive atmosphere, students may, in the process of evoking deep feelings from the past, naturally feel sadness, loss, and pain. My experience, however, both as a student and a leader in the course, is that the acts of writing and sharing with a sympathetic group seem to heal the wounds that are opened.

A man who is in a twelve-step recovery program dealing with painful childhood material told me that the weekend course in spiritual autobiography helped his own healing process, and that although he dug up painful material from the past, "not only did I find old pain I also found grace there, and that kept happening. I would somehow bump into some kind of grace when I went toward the hardest parts."

Of course, spiritual autobiography does not hold a therapeutic guarantee for everyone, and doubtless there will be occasions when people find that writing about painful memories is troublesome. Delving into one's deepest feelings is certainly a risk, but in my experience, the benefits far outweigh that pain. Everyone should feel completely free, however, to avoid what does not seem "ripe" or ready to come forth. People should not be made to feel they have to look for painful experiences, or deal with things they don't feel ready to explore.

There are many levels at which one can write spiritual autobiography, many metaphors for pain and joy, many ways to reflect without revealing things the individual feels are better left unsaid or unshared. One of the most fascinating spiritual autobiographies I have heard was written by a woman who wrote her whole story from the point of view of her shifting perceptions of nature and the natural world. When she finished reading, I had a rich sense of her journey, yet I knew not a single detail of her "personal" or private experience.

When I asked Reverend Scovel if he thought the spiritual autobiography course was a healing experience for people, he said "My off-the-cuff reaction is that I assume it is in some way healing, but that's too facile. I think it's a good experience, and any experience that's intrinsically good has a healing element. The question then is, where does it lead? It's possible for people to take all this religious or spiritual experience and process it into a kind of 'self-development' type mentality, which to my mind is really a 'going nowhere' kind of thing. I'm always asking, how does my story lead to 'our story'? I'm talking about identifying with the whole human venture."

Reverend Doss told me that "people who did this course were bonded to the group and to the church afterward. They tended to become more active, become the leaders of the church. I have heard people say it turned their lives around, that they changed the work they were doing as a result. An atheist who took the course began by being very challenging to the believers in the group, and although he didn't change his humanism, he became much more open to the believers, accepting the validity of their beliefs."

A therapist who took the last course I led at the Boston Center wrote me in evaluation that she felt "the group provided a safe way for most of the members to cope and feel connected." About half the class members have chosen to meet every month at members' homes to continue to share their experience, sometimes bringing additional pieces of writing, sometimes just discussing their latest projects, thoughts, and life experiences. Some of them wrote papers sharing what the course had meant to them five months after it ended. One woman told us:

> As you all know, the process of writing the autobiography required that we examine the events in our life from the view that last November and December's "balcony" [the time period of the course] offered. Although I must have known when I decided to do the class that it would provide me with an experience I was ready for and needed, amazingly I was at times overwhelmed by the intensity and clarity of the process.
>
> Simultaneously with the beginning of the class, I was led to read Carl Jung's autobiography, *Memories, Dreams,*

*Reflections,* which I found helped me enormously in approaching my own story, understanding my own story, and receiving the experience of having a veil lifted from my mind so that my vision was no longer as clouded as it had been in regard to family situations.

A close friend who shared many of my family situations gave me an issue of *The Yoga Journal.* It contained an article about dysfunctional families, Adult Children of Alcoholics (ACOA), the history of Alcoholics Anonymous, and suddenly I was reading about many of the experiences I had had in my own family.

Shortly afterward I was advised to attend some of the ACOA meetings, which I have been doing since February. I feel enormously fortunate and grateful that I have finally arrived at a place of understanding and nourishment, even though occasionally the sense of disbelief still hangs on— denial being such an amazing obstacle.

A man from that class wrote:

I truly believe there is an encouraging Spirit of God which inspires us to creative loving acts that work to our own good and the benefit of others. And often we never know what good we're doing except that our gift lives on in some fashion in the lives of others. That's why I marvel at what we all so courageously expressed. I feel blessed by your generosity, and have a tremendous and renewed respect for the tender hidden feelings and experiences of your lives.

This appreciation came as a bit of a surprise to me. As an artist, I'd have thought my sensitivity to the feelings and value in the experiences of others would have been a given but that's not necessarily true. Like my artistic talents, the ability to love the lives of others needs to be learned and practiced. So I thank you all for your training in this area. Your sharing has unlocked a door in my own growth and development that leads to even wider horizons and more significant expression of my own life.

The group which completed the most recent course at King's Chapel with a potluck supper agreed to meet again in six months, with each person pledged to bring food and a two-page paper on where their spiritual journey has taken them in that period. In the meantime, one of the members of that class wrote me her evaluation of the course.

The course was helpful because it helped me to rethink and refeel, and thus integrate those experiences, both positive and negative, that shaped the spirit of whom I am. It set me on the path of mending those feelings of alienation I had towards the church, and is thus freeing me to receive from the church spiritual nourishment. It also made me aware of all the areas of my life that do provide nourishment of the spirit. I hope I can more easily identify, when I am in the desert of life, what might help me, and also that I can keep myself nourished so I won't have to get to the level of starvation or thirst. So seldom in life do we get to tell our own story, or listen to someone else's real story. That was a deep experience.

# 4 How to Do It

As few as two and as many as fifty people can create some version of the course in spiritual autobiography. The only firm rule I would set about numbers is that no fewer than two people at a time should do the work of the course. In other words, don't do it alone. It's certainly possible to take the exercises and suggestions presented here, go home, and follow them in your own room with the door closed. I doubt that lightning would strike you down or the earth swallow you up, but I also doubt that you would get the full benefits of the experience without the participation of at least one other human being. You might miss the very essence of it.

Unless you are a lighthouse keeper or a forest fire watcher who lives alone in a tower, this should not prevent you from doing the course. Get a friend to do it with you. If you don't have a friend, here's a great way to make one: invite someone whom you'd like to know better to join you in a course of simple drawing and writing exercises that will help you both learn more about yourselves by writing your life stories.

*Doing the Course with One Other Person*

Scott took one of the weekend workshops I led in spiritual autobiography, and then used the basic material to do the course with Mike, a friend whom he knew from a twelve-step recovery program. Scott and Mike told me how it came about, and how they worked together.

"I had begun a writing course," Mike said, "but it wasn't what I wanted. After the third session the instructor kept some of us after class and said we hadn't 'found our voice' and harangued us with all kinds of questions to 'help us find our voice.' She asked me, 'Did you have a terrible childhood? Tell me all about it!' After that I bailed out. In one of our twelve-step meetings I discussed my frustration in wanting to share my writing with someone, but not in a critical setting."

Scott said, "Mike had this idea that he wanted to sit down with someone else and have the two people write for each other and then read to each other. At the time, I thought the idea was crazy. Then I took the spiritual autobiography workshop, and I said to Mike 'Hey, that's a great idea you had!' We started getting together at each others' apartments, and I'd give him one of the exercises from the workshop, then we'd both go off to different rooms, do the drawing, come back and discuss it, then we'd both go off and write. We were always within hollering distance, and I just said to Mike, 'Give me a holler when you're done.'"

Scott had wanted to continue the writing he had done in the weekend workshop I led in Cambridge, and found that working with Mike "provided a safe, good way for me to do it." Mike feels that working with another person "created a nice kind of pressure to do the writing," and he also found that "there's a safety in delving into deep feelings if I feel the trust of someone with me, listening to me, rather than writing alone."

"We read aloud to each other what we'd written," Mike went on, "but with the stipulation, which was very important to me, that we weren't required to read if we didn't want to read that particular piece. After my experience in the writing class I was dreading what Scott might say at first after I read, but it was fine. We respond more from our personal reaction rather than as a literary discussion or criticism."

Scott nodded, and gave an example. "Last week when we got together it was a nice summer evening so we went out to the Boston Common to read what we'd written. After Scott read, all I said was, 'I feel blue,' just to give him an immediate emotional response."

Mike explained that "We share a background from our twelve-step program where there are very clear guidelines about not giving advice, about being very respectful of another person and what they say, so we had some skills we'd developed through that and some understanding we didn't have to spell out, like we didn't have to say 'OK, I'm going to read something really sad and I don't expect you to respond by telling me what to do.' I think these are important guidelines to establish—that you don't want the other person to 'solve' anything for you, or take care of you, or whatever."

"In the twelve-step program, we never 'evaluate' another person's story," Scott added.

"There's a great safety in that," Mike said, "knowing initially we're not going to discuss this in depth, not going to try to take it apart and dissect it. We read and just wait for the other person's response, and the pause might be a long time, might seem to take forever, or it might be wham, right into it."

Scott said, "I recommend this course for anyone who's in a recovery program. Find a person who's in it with you and go and write these experiences that you don't have a chance to put down on paper otherwise. The exercises give a structure to the writing. Telling the story is very important, and there's something about writing it that's even more powerful."

As well as experiencing benefits in terms of both writing and personal growth, the two men found that a spiritual dimension naturally emerged from the work of the course.

Scott said, "I feel there's an essential spirituality in childhood, and it gets whittled away in adulthood, so simply going back to that world, as we do in this writing, is itself a spiritual act."

Mike was raised Catholic, left the Church, and converted to Lutheranism. He is now a member of a Lutheran church. "In a spiritual sense it was helpful to write about my memories of being a young child in the Catholic church. I find I can write about it now with some dark humor, and that's all right. It doesn't feel wrong or sinful to discuss church this way, it doesn't seem irreverent. I wrote a piece on sexuality and spirituality, about adolescence and growing up in the church. I not only remembered the pains of that, but I found I could go back without the anger I once felt, and appreciate the warmth and richness of the experience.

"Sometimes I sensed the spiritual just in the process of coming together," Mike continued, "in making time to write and share with each other, in being vulnerable in that way. In doing it I've had a sense of the—well, 'holy' is the word that comes to mind."

The manner in which Scott and Mike conduct their two-person course could serve as a guideline for anyone doing this work. Their experience also illustrates that the course can serve as a springboard for you to continue writing and exploring your spiritual autobiography.

*The Community of the Group*
While sharing with one other person can be a beneficial and satisfying experience, the community of a small group seems to provide the most congenial and supportive circumstance for doing the course in spiritual autobiography. My own experience in taking and leading the course is that ten to twelve people is ideal, and fifteen ought to be the maximum, simply because there's not enough time for everyone to read their papers with more than fifteen. Furthermore, the sense of community that comes from a small group getting to know one another begins to be diluted when enrollment rises above fifteen.

If you belong to a church or synagogue, you are already part of a community, and church members who enroll in a course on spiritual autobiography have a commonality of belief and background of faith to begin with, as well as a familiarity with their fellow worshipers. The gathering of the small group within the larger community intensifies natural bonds that are already there. Also, the setting of a church or temple is a place that is already regarded as a sanctuary, a safe place for people to assemble and share personal explorations.

While a setting within an already established religious community is ideal for doing this work, it is not essential. When I offered the course for the first time at the Boston Center for Adult Education, I worried that people with different backgrounds assembling at a "neutral" educational facility might not be able to establish the kind of community and trust necessary for the work. For the most part, I feel it succeeded, though I think that first class did not work as well as the one I did there the following year. I base that judgment on the fact that in the first class, only nine of fifteen people who originally enrolled did all the work of the course, completing the final eight-to-ten-page spiritual autobiography; the following year, all but one of the students completed the entire course and wrote the full autobiography.

Perhaps this was due in part to my uncertainty in leading the course for the first time, with people whom I hadn't known before and who had no connection with each other except a desire to take a course about writing one's spiritual autobiography. Another thing that didn't help that first course was the setting. The class was held in a cold, almost barren room around a long table like the one in the famous breakfast scene in *Citizen Kane,* and the distance between us sometimes seemed as great as that between Orson Welles and Ruth Warrick (Mrs. Kane). The next year I made a special request to hold classes in the library, a warm and intimate space whose atmosphere was much more conducive to a feeling of ease and familiarity as we gathered informally at two round tables.

In leading groups since then in a variety of settings around the country, I have been amazed at how quickly a sense of community arises in a group of people who may not have known one another before they walked into the room. Any initial stiffness or nervousness seems to dissipate when the participants pair off to share the drawing of the first exercise, explaining their drawings to each other. The animated look and sound of the room when this process begins is always a relief to me, as I can see and hear before me the coming together of a community.

At the beginning of any course or workshop, I ask everyone to introduce themselves by saying two or three sentences about why they chose to do this sort of program. If there is time, I pass out paper and crayons and ask each person to take fifteen minutes and "draw the present," whatever that means to them. Then each person explains their drawing as a way of introduction to the group.

When I say I "lead" this course rather than teach it, I am making an important distinction. I have taught a number of different courses in the past, in which I have presented information through lectures, discussion, and the criticizing and grading of papers. None of those methods are used in the course on spiritual autobiography. I "lead" the course in the sense that I present its structure, explain the exercises, and try to set a tone and atmosphere.

A feeling of trust and safety is essential, and I assure people that one of the rules of this work is "the right to reticence," which means that no one is required to do, say, draw, write, or share anything they don't wish to do. Anyone is free to "pass" on reading an assignment, and in each course one or two people may do that on some occasion, and ought to be made to feel comfortable in exercising that option. We also observe the rule of confidentiality, agreeing that nothing shared in the group will ever be discussed outside of it.

I feel that in presenting the course I am like a stage manager or set builder who puts up scaffolding for the presentation of people's life dramas. I introduce them with the honor to which they are entitled as humans engaged in a noble enterprise, and then I sit back and appreciate what happens as the individuals emerge in the special fullness of their own stories. Afterward I show my appreciation with a brief comment of recognition and acknowledgment. There is no time for lengthy group discussion, and only brief words of support from others are appropriate. I explain we are here for mutual support, not criticism, even of the "constructive" kind, which can too often lead to dissection rather than appreciation.

One need not have any particular training or expertise to be a leader. In a church or synagogue, the minister, priest, or rabbi who is already recognized as the spiritual leader of the community is the natural person to conduct the course. Reverend Scovel says it is a marvelous way for him as minister to get to know parishioners at a deeper level than is ordinarily possible. I know as a parishioner taking the course with him, it was a special benefit to be able to do the work with the minister as leader, for I felt I was conveying information I wanted him to know about my spiritual life and quest, and that there was a stronger bond between us as a result of the experience.

If for reasons of time commitment (meaning overcommitment, which is common among leaders of religious congregations) the minister, priest, or rabbi is unable to lead a course in spiritual autobiography at a particular time, there is no reason why a member of the congregation could not serve as the facilitator (that is what the leader really is in the course, one who helps forward the process or assists the progress of the course). Certainly no background or training in theology or writing is necessary. The most important qualities the leader can have for this work are respect for the individuality and worth of each participant, humility before the awesomeness of each person's life process, and appreciation of the gift of sharing it.

If you are not a member of any religious congregation, the course may appropriately be offered at any adult education center. (Most adult education centers seem open to ideas for new courses, and new people presenting them. You of course have to sell yourself as well as the course, and I know people who have done that with little or no previous experience, but simply through their enthusiasm and making a convincing case for the potential audience of such a program.) On the occasions I have led it at the Boston Center for Adult Education and at Interface, some students have enrolled who are active members of religious congregations. Most have at some point left formal affiliation with whatever organized religion they grew up with, but are seeking a way to explore the questions of their own spiritual life with other people on the same quest.

The course may also be conducted outside of any institutional setting, religious or secular, simply by a gathering of friends who take turns meeting at each others' homes. In such a situation, participants might also share the leadership of the course, taking turns in conducting the session on a particular evening. Perhaps the person who is host to the group when it meets at his or her home could also lead the exercises and discussion that evening.

The plan I am going to describe outlines what I think of as the "basic" spiritual autobiography course, as I first took it from Reverend Scovel at King's Chapel, and first taught it at the Boston Center for Adult Education. This course takes place in a series of eight evening sessions over the same number of weeks. The first four sessions are devoted to drawing exercises that evoke memories and lead to discussion, and the writing and reading of brief papers on varieties of spiritual experience. The last four sessions are devoted to reading and hearing the full eight-to-ten-page spiritual autobiography written by each student.

It is obviously impossible to write a full autobiography in a weekend or one-day workshop. In these cases, shortened versions of the basic course are used, with selected drawing exercises followed by discussion in pairs. The writing evoked by those exercises is done in class and read in the group at that time. Some students find that this writing in short time periods in the group is easier than going home and having a week to write a two-page paper on the subject. Both the eight-week format and the condensed weekend workshop or retreat have advantages and disadvantages. Both are worth doing. Even a one-day or half-day session can provide a taste of the experience, perhaps serve as the impetus for people to begin their spiritual autobiographies, and give them a new vantage point from which to look at their experience.

If you really want to do the course in spiritual autobiography, but perfectly good and logical reasons and circumstances seem to stand in the way, I urge you to look again at the possibilities. No matter how imperfect the situation, something good has come out of this work every time I have done it. Remember that these exercises and instructions are not set in stone, but can be altered and modified to suit the circumstances in which you are working.

If in doubt, go ahead with whatever you have to work with. If you don't have crayons, do the drawings with pencils; if you don't have a cozy, book-lined room, do it in someone's basement; if you don't have many people, do it with a few; if you have too many people, do it anyway; if you don't have the right kind of paper or bright enough lighting, or something for people to write or draw on that seems absolutely necessary, do it anyway. I did it once, under almost all those adverse circumstances, even though it went against all my rules and preconceived theories, and I've been happy about it ever since.

Here's the story of what happened, with written results as proof of my claim.

I had agreed to lead an evening introduction to spiritual autobiography at the Paulist Center in Boston, without first checking out the arrangements and the setting where the program would take place. The room was not what I expected at all. In fact, it wasn't really a room; it was the main sanctuary of the church. There was no writing surface unless you bent over and put the paper next to you on the pew, and tried to draw and write on that, which wasn't even a flat surface. The paper wasn't plain and white, as everyone knows is essential for drawing; it was some kind of green graph paper. There weren't any crayons or writing utensils; people had to use whatever pen or pencil they (hopefully) had with them. The lighting was so dim I didn't know if people would be able to see well enough to draw and write anyway. This was where I was supposed to lead an introductory evening session in spiritual autobiography.

There was a crowd of about forty-five people, which was exactly three times the size of what I felt was the maximum number for doing such a session with any kind of success. Even if anyone succeeded against all odds in doing the drawing exercise, and then the writing that it was designed to evoke, the only way they could read it so everyone else could be sure of hearing it was to come to the front of the sanctuary, stand at a lectern, and speak into a microphone: hardly a situation to put a person at ease for sharing a significant personal experience with a crowd of strangers!

This was all wrong, and I made it clear in no uncertain terms to the person who had made the arrangements. I wince in recalling how curtly I spoke to her—rudely, to be honest—expressing my displeasure to the point where I considered calling off the whole thing and telling everyone to go home. As the arranger (who has since become a friend) calmly tried to accommodate me and explained the circumstances that made the existing situation necessary, it dawned on me that when I had spoken to her originally I had not conveyed what I wanted, but assumed she could read my mind. As it became painfully obvious that I was responsible for the evening's circumstances, and forty-five people were sitting there in good faith waiting for something to happen, I realized that I'd better make do with what was at hand.

To my great relief, people were able to draw as they bent over spaces in the pews, and shared their drawings eagerly with their neighbors when they paired off. After that they wrote with quiet concentration under the dim sanctuary light, as if they weren't even bothered or didn't notice that all the conditions were less than perfect. I could not imagine, though, that anyone would be brave enough to come forward and read their personal experience into the microphone before a group of strangers. With faint hope I invited anyone to come up and share what they had written, and to my surprise and delight a woman raised her hand to volunteer.

Sirkka Barbour, a Finnish woman from the Beacon Hill Friends, said she had written an account of an experience from her own childhood during World War II. She came to the microphone and read this story.

## Night Errand

SIRKKA
BARBOUR

Abandoned into the arctic night, shoved out by the aunts of the children's home. Why couldn't the aunts have gone? They were adults. Unaccompanied by other friends. Snickered at with glee by the boys. See, you have to go, not us. Hah, hah.

A call had come that afternoon from a farm house, an urgent message for medicine. A child was seriously ill with diphtheria. There was no doctor in the village, no hospital, not even a public health nurse. But there was a white medicine cabinet with a red cross on the door high up on the wall in the aunt's room. Forbidden to look in, even to touch.

After supper there was a conference around the dining table. Who should be sent? No one wanted to go. No one. The aunts had duties and responsibilities. The big boys hadn't done their schoolwork. It was Sirkka and Berta, me and my friend, the two biggest girls. Behind all the instructions and encouragement from the aunts, and a feeling of relief and ill will from the boys, there was anxiety and guilt. Berta and I protested and objected. To no avail.

We were bundled and wound into coats and scarves and

mittens and caps. Only our eyes showed. The medicine package we were to guard with our lives: hold it tightly. Do not drop. Do not break. Do not open it. And when you get to the stricken house, knock on the door and deliver the package, but do not go in, for fear of infection. We would recognize the house by a lighted lantern outside the door.

Was it a kilometer or two or three? The house was at the other end of the village. It was a long walk. We clung to each other. Dogs barked and whined. It was cold and dark. Our breath stuck on our lips and stung going down to our lungs. We told stories to each other. We tried to laugh. No one was to be seen anywhere. Only snow crunching under our boots. But there was the moon, brilliant and shiny, its rays sending glitters over the snow and ice. Suddenly we were not abandoned after all. The moon accompanied us.

A glimpse of new worlds opened up that night for all of us when our group in the dimly lit sanctuary heard the story of a childhood spiritual experience of the woman from Finland.

# 5 First Exercise: Childhood

We begin at the beginning, with our earliest memories.

Before evoking that time and place through an exercise in drawing, I like to read a few short passages that I feel help convey a sense of the rich possibilities of the kind of writing we are preparing to do, and set a tone of confidence in the process. You may use these quotations or not, substitute others you like better, or go directly into the drawing exercise, whatever feels most appropriate. I believe these thoughts are relevant to any good writing, but especially to writing about childhood. The first is from one of my favorite books, a slim volume called *Letters to a Young Poet,* by Rainer Maria Rilke, in which the great poet advises an aspiring young writer about the craft and art he wishes to learn. Whenever people ask me about how to become a writer, I tell them to read these letters of Rilke.

Here is the poet's advice on beginning to write:

> Then try, like some first human being, to say what you see and experience and love and lose. . . . Save yourself from general themes and seek those which your own everyday life offers you; describe your sorrows and desires, passing thoughts and the belief in some sort of beauty—describe all these with loving, quiet, humble sincerity, and use, to express yourself, the things in your environment,

the images from your dreams, the objects of your memory. If your daily life seems poor, do not blame it; blame yourself, tell yourself that you are not poet enough to call forth its riches. . . . And even if you were in some prison the walls of which let none of the sounds of the world come to your senses—would you not then still have your childhood, that precious, kingly possession, that treasure-house of memories?

The reference to the "treasure-house of memories" reminds me of another passage that I think carries on and deepens Rilke's image. This is a dialogue between a student and master from the book *Zen Flesh, Zen Bones*.

> Daiju visited the master Baso in China. Baso asked: "What do you seek?"
> "Enlightenment," said Daiju.
> "You have your own treasure house. Why do you search outside?" Baso asked.
> Daiju inquired: "Where is my treasure house?"
> Baso answered: "What you are asking *is* your treasure house."
> Daiju was enlightened! Ever after he told his friends: "Open your treasure house and use those treasures."

The image of childhood as a "treasure house of memories," and the idea that each of us has the capacity not only to "open our treasure house" but to "use those treasures," are especially apt for the exercise we are going to do now.

Take a piece of blank paper and a supply of crayons or colored markers.

Draw a picture of your favorite room in the house you grew up in. If you grew up in more than one house, choose the one with the happiest memories. Choose the room in it with the happiest memories and best associations. If you regard all the houses you grew up in as sort of Charles Addams monster mansions with no redeeming memories, then draw a room you did like in the house of a relative (good old Aunt Mary's kitchen or Grandpa's den or Joey's rec room or the attic in

Helen's house with the trunk full of old clothes). One man in a class said he couldn't think of any pleasant rooms from his childhood and asked if he could do a picture of his backyard. Yes, that would be fine.

Most people don't have trouble thinking of at least one room from childhood with good and positive associations, but a few have a problem with it, and ought to be allowed and encouraged to think of some place that does have good memories for them, like their backyard, or a schoolroom, or maybe even the local drugstore, if that was a focal point and important place for the person. The point is to find a place in your past that you can use to evoke memories of that time in your life. Remember also that even if unpleasant memories come, they too can be "treasures," perhaps the most valuable treasures of all, especially when examined from the new perspective that may develop in this sort of exploration.

You may draw either a picture of the room (like a painting done with crayons) or a floor plan or diagram, showing everything you can remember: furniture, pictures on the wall, rugs, curtains, radios, TV set, toys, appliances, windows, doors, bookcases, books, record player, plants, fans, air conditioner, vases, pots, even pets (dog, cat, hamster, parrot), whoever and whatever you remember inhabiting the room.

Take twenty minutes to do the picture of the room. Think about it first, perhaps sketching it in with pencil. Then fill in everything you can think of. If you get stuck after the basic furniture, think of details. At the end of ten minutes or so, if the leader sees some people who seem to have run out of things to add to the room, suggest some possibilities by asking questions. What was your favorite meal that might have been on the kitchen table you drew? (I have drawn the bowls of chili I loved at my childhood supper table.) What were your favorite TV or radio programs at that time? You could list those at the side, with a line pointing to the radio or TV set. What were your favorite books? List some at the bottom of the paper, with an arrow pointing to the bookcase. Whose photographs were on the wall? Draw the tree you saw when you looked out the window of the room. Draw a person who often came into the room—mother, friend, brother. Put in everything you can think of, large or small, important or peripheral—it is all part of the picture of your own past, your treasure house of memory that can be transformed into story.

After twenty minutes, everyone should pick a partner and go off in pairs to explain to each other the room they have drawn. Each person should take ten minutes to explain what they drew, what's in the room. The other person may ask questions about the picture, or about how its artist describes it, to get the fullest sense of what it was like being in that other person's room at that time of his or her life. At the end of ten minutes the leader of the session asks the partners to switch, so that the other person explains their picture and answers questions about it.

Part of the value of the exercise is in the sharing of the picture of the room. In telling about what they drew, people learn more about that time and place, as memory is deepened and more memories are evoked. It is also a marvelous way for the people sharing their pictures to get to know one another.

The leader should announce when the second ten-minute period is over, and everyone returns to the group. In the next part of this exercise, everyone writes about a childhood spiritual experience. Drawing the favorite room from childhood and sharing it with another person evokes many memories of that time, but you don't necessarily have to write about one of the memories that came specifically from that exercise; nor do you have to write about something that happened in or is connected with the room you drew. The important thing is that your childhood has been evoked by the drawing, and you have more access to it now.

The next task is to think of something that happened in childhood (defined loosely as the time before adolescence) that you might consider a spiritual experience. It doesn't have to have occurred in a church or synagogue or any kind of formal place of worship, or be specifically religious in nature, like a baptism or confirmation or incident at Sunday School, though it may be any of those things if that's what you want to write about.

Rather than trying again to define "spiritual," the leader may wish to read a few short passages as examples of material considered to be spiritual, and which have been written from childhood experience. Sometimes I read a passage from the Anthony Powell novel *The Kindly Ones*. The passage tells of the narrator returning to the house he grew up in, and describes the memory of feelings he had when he lived there as a child: "Here, among these woods and clearing, sand and fern, silence and the smell of pine brought a kind of release to the heart, together with a deep-down wish for something, something more than battles, perhaps not battles at all; something realised, even then, as nebulous, blissful, all but unattainable: a feeling of uneasiness, profound and oppressive, yet oddly pleasurable at times, at other times so painful as to be almost impossible to bear."

I like this passage because it describes a kind of feeling I think of as spiritual, though it is not connected to a specifically religious activity or experience. I feel it liberates people from too narrow a definition of "spiritual."

I also like to read something from one or two papers people have written in these courses about a childhood experience. Hearing this work is helpful, since it is not the work of professional writers, and indicates not only the range of spiritual experience, but also the ability of people much the same as the ones now gathered to draw on their own personal experience and write from it in a way that is expressive and illuminating.

The leader may read from papers I include in this section, as well as from his or her own favorite books or stories, in order to provide examples of a childhood spiritual experience. There should not be a lot of further discussion about definitions of it after reading the examples. Tell each person to take pen or pencil and paper and find a place to sit and write. They will have forty minutes to think about and write their own childhood spiritual experience. If most people are finished after thirty minutes, the leader may obviously call a halt. Forty minutes is the maximum amount of time I have given for this writing exercise, and with the exception of a few people who got started on stories of epic proportions, this has been ample.

If this is a once-a-week evening class, it should end after the writing. Ask people to bring what they wrote to be read at the following class. If this is a day-long or weekend workshop, take a break, and then assemble again to have participants read what they have written.

When the class assembles again to read the pieces they have written—whether it is the same day or the following week—the leader should guide this important part of the experience with full attention and gentle, compassionate support.

In terms of reaction and comment, less is more. When a person is finished reading, the leader need not comment immediately, may take a few moments of silence, then might ask a sympathetic question about some aspect of the story told, or make a brief comment of appreciation of what has been shared. I always thank the person who has read. Others in the class may comment or question in the same spirit (and with similar brevity), but not in any challenging or dissecting manner, never evaluating or giving advice.

The leader sets the tone of response, and I have never had to ask anyone to restrain their comments or reactions. The respect is almost inherent in the process, for the writing that is shared is so authentic and moving that it naturally elicits a response that honors the experience and its author. As one man who took the course explained to some others in a training session, "When people are reading their papers to the group, you know that is 'holy ground.'"

The following papers illustrate the results of all the exercises and assignments (Childhood, Adolescence, and Friend/ Mentor/Guide) and were written in the courses and workshops I led in many different places, from Boston to Seattle, over the past two years. Some were written at home during the week-long interval between classes; others were written on the spot, in a day-long or weekend workshop or retreat when only from half an hour to forty-five minutes were allowed for the writing. All are true reflections of the spirit, and I honor them as such.

In leading the course, I do these exercises again myself, and I find that they always unlock new doors to my treasure house of memory. This is not a course one can simply do once and then it is over. I have drawn different rooms in the house I grew up in, and I have drawn the same room over many times; each time I discover something new in it, something that was there but which I had forgotten, or something that happened in it that returns with great power and clarity.

The first time I ever did the exercise, when I took the course at King's Chapel, I drew the living room of the house I grew up in, and this is what I saw: "First there is light. My father is playing the small foot-pedal organ in the living room of our house in Indianapolis and my mother and I are singing along with him that 'in the dark streets shineth the everlasting light,' and I feel a deep and quiet thrill, a tingling in the skin, for I know this season and its music are sacred and so is the light described in the song and even the light from the lamp outside in our own dark street that shines in the frosted pane of the front room window."

Having drawn the sketch of that house, I felt I could look inside its windows and see the beginning of my own journey, hear the music and conversation, feel the emotions. So will you, just as have these people whose stories follow.

## Heat

ALAN
BODNAR

My mother always warned me not to let anyone know we were poor—not poor in the sense of not having enough to eat or having to wear shabby clothes, but poor enough to live in an apartment without heat or a telephone. Even in the fifties, heat and a telephone were considered necessities by most of our friends and acquaintances. Mom seemed to believe that if someone knew you lived without the comforts that most people take for granted, then at best they'd look down on you and at worst they wouldn't want to have anything to do with you. I suppose that for the most part, I heeded her admonitions, but of course your best friends always knew the truth and it didn't seem to matter. How could you conceal the fact that you didn't have a phone from a kid who played at your house and saw first hand the curious way that you made contact with the outside world? That's where the dance hall across the street comes in, with its public phone booth outside the door. We gave out the number of this telephone to a select few of our friends with instructions to call, let the phone ring three times, hang up, and dial again. That was the signal that the call was intended for one of us, and the rest was just a matter of going across the street to answer it. Of course the system only worked in the summer when we used the living room which faced the dance hall and had the screens in place. Otherwise it was too cold. For the rest of the year, we could always rely on a neighbor, and there was never a problem making a call from the phone booth. Today, thirty years later, our house has been leveled for a parking lot, but the dance hall and the phone booth are still thriving.

The matter of heating evokes more complicated memories, and, along with so many other aspects of my childhood, contributes to my belief that spirituality exists in the most commonplace details of everyday life. The only source of heat in our house was a wonderful old brown-and-cream-colored kitchen stove. The gas jets on the surface were always burning through the cold New Jersey winters, and when the mercury really plunged the oven did an admirable job of warming the room. As for the rest of the house, the living room was sealed off: a room-sized icebox thawed only for special occasions like Christmas morning. At those special times, a kerosene stove supplied the necessary heat as well as the unfortunate smell of a tanker's boiler room. But the smell that I recall most clearly is the fragrance of the orange peels that my mother would place on the top of the heater to mask the undesirable aroma of the kerosene. Not even the frankincense of the Magi could have smelled so sweet as the skins of those oranges that my mother offered for her family on the parlor stove.

The bedrooms in winter were frigid, but I was always warm and cozy under layers of down comforters. Leaving that snug nest when the alarm rang for school was the real challenge. It was my father who made it possible, getting up an hour before my mother and me and turning on the kitchen stove. I remember very clearly the muffled sounds he made shuffling around the kitchen, getting ready for work and stirring his ever-present cup of hot tea. The reassuring clink of spoon against cup, metal clapper on ceramic shell was as spiritual as any church bell, though I probably didn't realize it until I became a father myself.

———

## A Deck of Cards

DONNA
JOHNSON

On a warm summer night, which seemed excessively long to me at the age of four, I was in the quiet of my room while my parents played cards with friends downstairs in the living room. I had already spent time trying to read a book, by holding it on the floor in front of the door to my bedroom, using the hallway light coming from beneath the door as illumination.

Then, still feeling left out, I went carefully out of my room to sit high enough up on the stairs so as not to be seen. I could hear their adult voices and laughter. I yearned for those things and the light. Though I thought myself unseen, I was discovered by my mother and she gave me a deck of cards to play with in my room.

Back in there by myself, part of me no longer felt quite so left out, while part of me continued to have a growing urge to make a statement—to experience my existence the way it felt the adults did theirs.

I took the deck of cards to my bedroom window, which was open and overlooked our driveway. With a rush of sensation that I can still feel, I took each card, bit down on it, and then dropped it out the window. I remember clearly what it was like to bite into a card, feel it give, and then see the lasting impression I had left. Dropping it outside linked me with a world in which I was too small to be included, and made my entry into it an act of defiance, a forced entry.

When I ran out of cards, I went to bed, now sleepy, having succeeded in making my mark on the world.

————

## From My Room

ANONYMOUS

When I was a young child, I loved to look out my bedroom window at the parking lot next door. I lived in a gray two-family house in the center of town and the parking lot was in back of all the stores. From my room on the second floor I thought I could see the whole world, since it seemed that everyone came to Woolworth's or the First National during the day. I loved looking out, especially because no one knew I was there. Leaning on my windowsill, I felt a little special, watching what cars people drove or how many bags they carried. Seeing so many people was exciting.

Something strange always happened, though, once the

people started to go home and the stores closed for the day. The parking lot would slowly quiet down. As the cars left, I realized that everyone was going home to eat supper. I felt a bit sad as I saw the last cars leave. They usually belonged to the people who worked in the stores. Once the yellow car under my window left, I knew the day was over. The man who sold shoes at Filene's was always the last one to go home.

By then, the quiet was bigger than any quiet I had heard. It seemed to grow, and as it did, I felt like a different person. I was part of another world, a larger one with no people or cars. I was suddenly aware of the pine trees and the grass that grew in front of the parking lot, by the entrance. Most of all, I was aware of a huge silent sky covering everything. I felt a sense of something which would always be there, a quiet over the world, including me. I was only an observer of the parking-lot life with all the people, but this silent world had a place for me, a natural place. I felt no different from the grass or trees, or even the clouds or birds. I felt that someone knew I was there.

---

## At Christmas

SUSANNE WISSELL

This year, I am eleven. Christmas will be, I am sure, as present-filled as it has been in the past, but there will be a difference. My father isn't living at home this year; he will arrive on Christmas morning. He will be a guest in our home, someone who, I now feel, has sides to him I did not know before, and whom I may not want to know. It is easy to lose the feeling of Christmas when you feel you have lost someone you love.

My best friend Shelley and I are going Christmas shopping today. The store is hot; we can feel our necks and arms perspire, and our sweaters sticking to our bodies make us itch.

Shelley tries to pay for a yellow shirt for her brother; she stands for fifteen minutes on one line before the cashier screams she will have to go to another line if she wants to pay cash. After five stores, all the stuff looks the same and I am sickened by the sounds, the smells, the sights of Christmas. We are hungry, maybe for more than lunch. We are beginning to wonder, "What is Christmas about anyway?"

All the restaurants in the shopping center are packed. We finally get a table at the greasy diner where most people who like good food wouldn't choose to eat their lunch. We don't have much money left, so we carefully select our food according to what we can afford to pay.

The waitress looks like any diner waitress. She has brown hair caught in a net; she's tall and thin and looks like a giraffe sticking out of that silly short skirt they make her wear. When we look up at her, she smiles. She actually takes her time in getting our order and smiles, no—beams at us! We are amazed, because we realize she is the first person who has smiled at us the entire morning.

I spill my milk, a white river flowing across the table, falling slowly over the edge, flooding the floor. Shelley groans. We are certain now the waitress will turn surly, maybe even make us leave the restaurant. She returns to the table and cleans it with a sponge; someone else mops the floor. She is cheerful, saying, "These things happen, you know; nobody's perfect."

Perfect. That is what Christmas used to be, when I was little, when Dad was home, when my parents made Christmas for me. What the heck did they expect from me, anyway? I'm only a kid. What can I do to make Christmas—what can I give?

She returns once more to give us our bill. She says, "Now don't you hurry, you relax and enjoy your lunch. And have a very Merry Christmas." We stare open-mouthed at each other, amazed. When we take out the money we have just enough to pay the bill and eleven cents left over. And then we remember the tip. We have only eleven cents for the person who smiled when she might have growled at us during the rush and frenzy of the season.

We place the eleven cents on the table with a note which says, "Please forgive us for having only eleven cents to give you. You were the only person who gave us any Christmas cheer today. Thank you and have a Merry Christmas."

Outside the diner we look back through the window and watch our waitress clear our table, pick up the eleven cents and read our note. She places the eleven cents in her pocket and she smiles—a broad, beautiful smile which spreads across her face and through her body, shining out in the way in which she clears our soup bowls and in the way in which she walks toward the next table. We watch her greet her next customer, and we know she is still smiling because it is reflected back from her customer's face.

---

## Northern Woods

### LINDA

When I was between six and eight years old, my family took vacations in Ontario, Canada, despite the fact that my mother said we didn't have the money. She said, however, that it was worth the expense if my father could relax and get himself together. I don't know if it helped my father, for the worst days were to come—but it helped me, a rather serious, worried child. I felt a great release and acceptance in the Northern woods and I have to call it a spiritual experience because it held me in the moment so totally that I let go of all past and future worries.

When I meditate today, I still try to bring back the memory of the haven I found as a seven-year-old child. This haven was a quiet place around the bend of the lake about a quarter of a mile from the cottages. A huge boulder was perched on a mossy carpet beneath the pine trees. This hard rock beckoned me to sit. I could see from that location the ripples that the wind created over the water. I felt the warm rays of sunshine coming through an opening in the pine trees. I heard the continual lapping of the waves hitting the shore. I watched the waves swirl around another boulder in the water. This simple common experience renewed me.

It demanded nothing of me except that I come and sit quietly and breathe. It helped me to bear the feeling of aloneness. I felt helped by this rock, this place—no less or more than what was around me.

It was good to feel eternity in my bones and that no matter what happened in my family, there was a bigger world to sustain and hold me.

I went there often, in many states of mind. I still go to that rocky place in my memory. I always felt it was the experience of God.

# 6  Second Exercise: Adolescence

The hymn played at my baptism when I was eleven years old was, ironically (and probably appropriately), the one I most disliked. The words began "Have thine own way, Lord / Have thine own way / Thou art the potter, I am the clay. . . ." It went on to ask God to "mold me and make me" however he wanted. This angered and frightened me. I wanted to have *my* own way. I simply wanted God to help me get it. With this conflict brewing (me vs. God!) I "entered the fury of adolescence," as I put it in describing that era of my life in my book *Returning*.

Adolescence is almost by definition a time of rebellion. It is a time when we question our parents, our teachers, the rules we've been given, the religion we were brought up to believe in. It is a crucial and often tumultuous time in our journey.

Rebellion is part of faith. It is not an aberration, but a natural part of the process of spiritual growth and development. It is healthy and human to question what we've believed in. After such times of testing we return to faith in a more personal and meaningful way, not as something we've only been given, but as something we've wrestled with, challenged, and earned. This may happen more than once on our journey, and may even be a regular or cyclical part of it. Usually the first time it happens is in adolescence, when we are flexing our minds as well as our muscles, exploring and questioning everything in hopes of discovering who we are.

In my own adolescence, before I discovered much about who I was, I discovered who I was not. I was not an athlete. I was not a football or basketball star, or even a player who could make the high school teams. This was a terrible blow, for I idolized the ballplayers, the heroes of my childhood and youth whose feats drew the cheers of the crowd, the admiration of men, and the love of women. I strove mightily to earn such accolades, putting my adolescent heart and soul to the test—only to fail.

My failure became clear my freshman year in high school, when I set as my goal the conquest of the mile run. In those days that meant running it in something less than six minutes. (Today, many healthy grandmothers are able to accomplish that feat or better it.) I chose the mile, that mythic distance, because I had heard a talk from our high school principal, who said that while many boys did not possess the talent or coordination or natural ability to excel at team sports, every boy could become a runner, by sheer dint of effort. Running, too, could earn one a uniform, ribbons, a letter, and even some cheers, so I set out to try.

At dusk every evening I would change into my old clothes and go over to the nearby high school track to practice. I ran the four laps that constituted the mile, barely making the distance intact, but making it nonetheless. I even saved up money and bought a stopwatch to time myself. Running my best race, I found when I staggered over the finish line that I had run the mile in just over seven minutes.

I was undaunted. I ran my heart out, and a few weeks later, timed myself again. I had managed to reduce my time by two seconds, to seven minutes flat. I had failed to break the seven-minute mile. Despite the inspiring words of the principal, I concluded that my flat feet or my flabby middle or a combination thereof were unsurmountable obstacles to my dreams of athletic glory.

As so often happens in life, however, my failure opened the door to a new and more meaningful opportunity: I stopped running, and started writing about other people running. I became a reporter for my high school paper, *The Shortridge Daily Echo,* and a correspondent for the local morning paper, *The Indianapolis Star.* The first time I walked into the sports department of *The Star,* heard the clicking of the press service wires, and saw the men whose bylines I knew hunched over their typewriters, pounding out new stories, I knew I was home. This door opened onto the deeply satisfying work of my whole life.

Looking back at our adolescence helps immensely in discovering who we are now and how we got to this point. Our exercise to evoke this period of the past is either to draw a picture of the way you saw yourself as an adolescent, to draw a picture of the way you saw God as an adolescent, or to draw a picture of both. Follow the same procedure of drawing and then sharing as in the first exercise.

Another tool for evocation of adolescence is a questionnaire, created by Reverend Scovel, which helps in bringing back the feelings and experience of the teen years. This may be completed in class before writing the paper, or distributed to participants to complete at home and discuss at the next session. Here is the questionnaire:

*Questions about Adolescence*

THE REVEREND CARL SCOVEL

Whom did you want to be like?

Whom did you loathe?

When did you first have to take a stand as an adolescent?

What choices did you have, and what choices did you not have?

What did you think of yourself?

What did you wish that someone could have told you at the time?

Did you like your father, and why?

Did you like your mother, and why?

What did your family talk about at dinner?

What books made a great impression on you?

When did you first leave home for a long time?

How did you earn money?

What day of the week did you like best?

At age fourteen, what were your convictions and your worries?

What was your first big disillusionment with an adult?

When, if ever, did you break with your church? Did that bring a feeling of depression or exhilaration?

What did you put in place of God?

When did you first feel like an adult?

Do you remember any experiences of deep faith or conviction or peace?

What were your friends like?

How were you hurt?

What were the powerful words at that time?

Sometimes I have asked people to answer the questionnaire, then pair off and share their adolescent experiences. Sometimes I have asked everyone in the group to take turns talking about their answers to one of the questions, for instance, "What was your favorite day of the week?" or "What were the powerful words at that time?"

Before writing a paper on an adolescent spiritual experience the leader should tell everyone that while rebellion is a common theme of that time of life, it is not necessary to write about rebellion (any more than it is necessary to write a childhood spiritual experience set in the room of the house you drew in the exercise). Feel free to write about whatever strikes you most deeply as a spiritual experience of your adolescence.

---

*An Open Letter to God*

ELEANOR JANE MILLER

So, where were you, huh?
I mean it
I want to know
what you were doing
while I was in high school

I've got a right to know,
don't you think?
or is the information locked away
with the truth about Lee Harvey Oswald
and the appearance of the Blessed Mother at Fatima

seriously,
do you expect me to believe
you kept yourself from me
for my own good?

Specifically,
I want to know how you could permit
Sister Mary Evelyn
to tell Trish Mulligan's mother
not to let her hang around with me
did it occur to you to say something to the good sister,
put her on the path so to speak?

And what about that all-girls Catholic school?
couldn't you have rigged it so that someone else
won the scholarship?
it's a well-known fact that girls like me
need well-rounded educations
that include boys

Speaking of boys
it's time you told me why my first boyfriend was thirty-four
couldn't you have stopped me,
pulled me aside and said something like,
"I don't think he's the one, kiddo; trust me"
I didn't hear you say anything
Am I right?

Another thing
how could you let Grammy move in with us?
I mean you are omniscient
and you knew she didn't like me
but into my house she came
chipping away at my childhood
belief in love

I also want to know why you put me into that family
without even a road map
you know I had nothing in common

with those strange people called
mom, dad, brother, sister

last
but not least
(and I know this may seem trite)
I have to know
why Loretta was chosen prom queen
instead of me
you must have known she didn't deserve it
just because her date's best friend played in the band
and they got to do the voting

What I really want to know, you see,
is why others got, and I didn't

I hope I haven't overstepped my bounds
in asking this crucial question

    Yours very sincerely,
    Eleanor Jane Miller

———

## Quarantine

JOHN

When I was eleven or twelve, I came into the bedroom I shared with my brother Jim and found my mother crumpled on her side on the floor. "Mom, what . . . ?" I said. "I'm all right," she said. "I just felt a little dizzy." She stirred and got up and walked out across the hall into my parents' bedroom, closing the door. I felt a little dizzy, too.

Jim and I got scarlet fever. A man from the city health department came and nailed a red sign on the front door with big black letters: QUARANTINE. My mother said scarlet fever was worse than measles or chicken pox: it could make you blind. We would have to stay in bed two weeks with the shades down. We played the radio and told cowboy stories. My mother brought our meals up on trays and came at other times to take our temperature and give us medicine with a spoon. My father stood at the door in the early evening and late at night asking how we were and saying, "It won't be long now."

Sometime later my mother got sick and was in the bedroom with the door closed. Jim and I could not see her until the next day. She lay in bed, pale. "I was going to have a little brother or sister for you," she said, 'but it wasn't meant to be. I went up and down the stairs a lot, you know, when you were sick." We didn't know what to say. She didn't say anything more. One morning she was in the spare bedroom, next to mine, with Mabel, my father's cousin. Mabe had come to take care of my mother and cook. "I can never tell Roger to do anything," my mother said. "I can only ask him." "He was always like that," Mabe said.

When I was thirteen, my mother had a baby boy in the hospital. He slept in her arms, with a lot of hair on his head.

A few years later she woke up Jim and me one night; she had her overcoat on. "It's time to go to the hospital. Just stay home from school with Tommy." We couldn't go see her as we did when Tommy was born. "The baby isn't good yet," my father said the next day. He answered the phone that evening. "Oh . . . well . . . I see . . . I see." When he hung up he was crying. "I don't have *any* luck, I don't have *any* luck!" "What happened?" I said. "It died!" he shouted. My mother was in bed at home for a week. I walked past her bedroom, I heard her crying. "Mabe, to think he could do it while I was in the hospital . . . in the hospital." Somehow I knew what she meant. I just knew. I knew he had been with a woman.

---

*Senior Prom*

ALAN
BODNAR

It was as I recall a beautiful day in May—warm but not too warm, the sky was a bright blue and the fresh scent of new grass and tulips drifted through the open window in Sister Maria's Latin class. I had loved the orderliness of Latin from that day in my freshman year when I conjugated my first verb. Now I was a senior and the subject was Virgil's epic poem of Aeneas. Latin was still one of my favorite subjects but today I just couldn't keep my mind on the hero returning from Troy. Tonight was the senior prom and we were being dismissed early so that we could make all of the necessary preparations for the big event. Just ten minutes more of Virgil, then a special mass for the seniors and we'd be on our way. They were always having special masses for something or other at Catholic high school. The last one was for President Kennedy, hastily arranged on the same afternoon he had been shot. That was a time of shock, sadness and profound disillusionment in our belief that we and the forces of good everywhere were invulnerable. Today was very different from that day in spirit, mood, and even the weather.

The bell rang, and after returning to homeroom to gather our belongings we filed across the street to the gothic stone church with the curious stained glass window inscribed, "Our lady of the Bronx. Pray for us." The mass was beautiful—inspirational but not too long. Surely God had arranged this perfect day for our class and it was only proper to thank him for it. Just when we thought we could leave, however, our principal, Sister Mary Assunta, took her place at the pulpit. "Before you go, boys and girls," she intoned, "I have just a word or two to say about tonight's prom. This is a wonderful time of your lives and we want you to enjoy yourselves. But first I'd like to tell you a sad but true story."

Uh-oh, I thought. This was the standard opening for one of Sister Assunta's cautionary tales. As we sat back in the pews, our principal told us about a pair of high school sweethearts who, on their way home from the prom, pulled over to the side of the road and, letting passion get the best of them, engaged in an Impure Act. "We don't know what they were thinking," droned the good nun, "or the state of their immortal souls at the time, but while they were parked, an eighteen-wheeler came barreling around the curve and smashed into the lovers' car, killing them both instantly. Need I say more?"

Certainly not to us. My classmates and I, having completed nearly twelve years of Catholic education, knew the moral of the story. Some years later, when I repeated the tale to a public school friend, he got a different message—something about driving to a more secluded and protected place before engaging in any impure acts.

Our dear principal was obviously a blood relative of the grammar school nun who taught us how to examine our consciences. Each of the Ten Commandments, she explained, can be broken in ways that constitute serious or mortal sin, and less serious venial sin—each of the Commandments, that is, except numbers Six and Nine, which have to do with sexuality. Any violation of those Commandments is automatically mortal. Much good in my life has come from my Catholic education, but I am a practicing Catholic today only because I have slowly and painfully learned to understand that the real message of the Church was not always taught in school. Though feelings of guilt about one thing or another still make me want to go dodge eighteen-wheelers, I am beginning to realize that I can learn more of God from the memory of that beautiful spring day of the prom with its gentle tulip-scented breezes and the timeless mystery of the mass than from all the tales of terror told by well-meaning but misinformed teachers and spiritual guides.

———

## No Escape

PAT AHERN

The high school corridors would become noisy, crowded, and somewhat disorderly in between classes. Because of all the pushing, entrances, exits, and large numbers of students, it would often take several minutes to get to the end of a hall. It was difficult to get a head start, stay ahead, or simply to walk in a straight uninterrupted line. But this is exactly what I tried to do—I tried to hurry, to push my way along, to stay ahead and get to my next class as quickly as I possibly could. I did this often, but I am thinking of one particular time, a period of time, the length of which I do not remember—several months?—between my fifth and sixth class each day. I was trying to run because I was being followed and wanted to escape my pursuers: classmates who chased me out of the classroom and down the corridor.

Even now, I cannot say for certain why I was being chased or exactly how it started. I do know why I was laughed at and talked about in class—that was because I could not see well enough to read the blackboard, hit the ball, or sometimes even recognize people. I often felt embarrassed and awkward because of this and, although I did not identify it as such then, frightened and sometimes angry. I tried to hide my difficulties but the moments when I could not turned into occasions for laughter and jokes for some of my classmates. I was not an adolescent for long before I was thought of, and treated as, someone very different from them. Some even became cruel. Sometimes their cruelty took an extreme form. This was one of those times.

I do not remember a starting day, or an ending day (the end of the school year, perhaps?), but suddenly it was happening, and once it started it seemed never to let up. I have tried to forget, but cannot forget, their loud voices, harsh laughs, crude questions and gestures, and their overwhelming physical strength. That they seemed to be so much stronger, and that there were more of them than of me, frightened me the most. Their original reason for not liking me seemed to be lost in some kind of madness (at least that is what I think of it as now) for they had stopped bothering me about what I could and could not see. They simply would not leave me alone, in class or out, until our ways parted halfway down the corridor.

My only concern was to survive. I was too embarrassed to tell anyone, too scared to fight back, and too confused to know even within myself what was happening to me. I thought that if I could just get through it I would be all right. As long as no one knew, I could pretend that it had not happened. I managed to escape a few times by making excuses to leave the class early (which involved fabricating a story for the teacher to account for my whereabouts—risky, so I could not do it often). One time I changed my route and left the room by the other door—that worked for one day. The next day one of my pursuers was waiting for me there. I was defeated, and remember well the sinking, helpless feeling I had as I nearly ran, trapped and trailed, down three flights of stairs—the only place to go in my attempt to avoid the long corridor. There was no real escape. Not until it ended.

I do not consider this to be a religious experience, since by religious I think of those times that have been in some way revealing, insightful, deepening. In order to survive, to go on with my life, I did not allow myself to feel, to talk about it, to cry about it, or to react in any emotional way to it. I pushed my feelings back harder and harder until there were none there. Until, I know now, some part of me, the part that had feelings and emotions, the religious part, was gone. I hid the feelings, but the experiences lodged themselves strongly in my memory and did not go away.

No, it was not a religious experience. What is religious about it now is my effort to accept its place in my memory and to understand its meaning in my life.

# 7 *Third Exercise:*
# *Friend/Mentor/Guide*

Every Christmas during my childhood I saved up money to give presents to my family, and also to send a contribution to Father Flanagan's Boy's Town. It was the first charity to which I ever donated money, and I think perhaps I was unconsciously reserving a room at Boy's Town in case things got too bad with my often warring parents. What a fabulous place it sounded like to a nine-year-old kid: a whole "town" of nothing but boys, presided over by one kindly "Father," played in the movie by Spencer Tracy.

What first drew me to the institution, though, and served as a powerful and reassuring symbol in my young life, was the picture in the Boy's Town ad appealing for funds, which ran in many national magazines in those days (the 1940s). I first saw it in a copy of my own favorite magazine, *Boy's Life,* and was immediately riveted by the picture of two shabbily dressed boys in the snow, one carrying the other on his back, and saying, "He's not heavy, Father—he's my brother."

I didn't have any brothers or sisters, but I already had good friends, from school and my neighborhood and the Cub Scouts (I was a proud member of Den 6 of Troop 90). I already knew I could trust and rely on guys like Jerry Burton, whom I met in kindergarten when we both shared the indignity of being sunflowers (yuk) in a class play, and Dicky Warne, whom I sat next to in the first grade at School 80 and later shared a tent with at Camp Chank-tun-un-gi when we were Boy Scouts. I knew I would have lugged either one of them through a blizzard to the safety of Boy's Town, and they'd have done the same for me.

I feel blessed by the good friends I've had throughout all the different stages of my life, and I know I could never have progressed through those stages without the help of those boys and girls, men and women, teachers and professors, editors and bosses, ministers and mentors, who gave me support, love, friendship, advice, understanding, scrambled eggs, loans of money, recommendations, places to sleep, rides, tickets, instruction, constructive criticism, praise, handclasps, and hugs.

I can't imagine a spiritual journey without the help of other people along the way. In my first class in spiritual autobiography at King's Chapel, I wrote about how such a friend had helped me at a sensitive time, and I included this story in my book *Returning*:

> My first day at Camp Chank-tun-un-gi I was so nervous and "green" that I couldn't even perform the simple task of unrolling my brand-new official Boy Scout sleeping bag on the upper bunk assigned to me. As I fumbled with the simple knots and zippers, in walked Jack Hickman, leader of the Hawk Patrol of my own Troop 90, who was a year older than I was and already a respected veteran of a whole summer at camp.
>
> I was terrified that he would not only laugh at me, but would spread the word that I was such a dumb rookie I couldn't get my sleeping bag unrolled. Instead, he quietly helped me get the damn bag properly laid out in official fashion on my top bunk, ready for inspection. Even more amazing, when I stammered out my embarrassed thanks, instead of bawling me out or making fun of me, he said with the staunch sympathy of a comrade, "That's OK— these sleeping bags are pretty tricky." I learned from Jack, to my surprise and relief, that to be a "Big Man" you did not have to ridicule the ineptitude of others, that respect

and understanding and even gentleness were not signs of weakness, but might in fact be indications of confidence and strength. (I also felt then that I had a friend for life, and I was right.)

There is another, darker piece I have read in these courses which some students have appreciated as an indication of how a friend can be a crucial, perhaps even lifesaving element in a time of crisis. This is from a novel I wrote called *Going All the Way,* about two young men who come home from the Korean war to try to start their lives and "find themselves" in the 1950s. Sonny Burns is a shy, chubby, introverted fellow who seems an unlikely buddy for Gunner Casselman, the star broken field runner of the high school football team, yet the two young men have much in common, and become true friends. In this scene, it is the bleak morning after Sonny has cut his wrist with a razor blade over suffering the humiliation and despairing frustration of not being able to consummate a sexual liaison with the girl of his dreams.

"What is it, man?" Gunner asked gently. "What's up?"
Sonny set his drink down on the coffee table, unbuttoned his left sleeve, and rolled it back, exposing the bandage. Gunner saw what it was, and he reached out and held Sonny's hand, squeezing it hard. His eyes got that look of staring into an atom blast, and he started shaking his head and saying softly, "No, man, that's not it, that's not the way. It isn't, man, it really isn't. I tell you, no, it's not."
He stood up and started pacing back and forth, saying, "We gotta do something, we gotta figure something out. We gotta get outa here."
Sonny just sat and watched him, unable to speak or think.
Gunner suddenly stopped and made the pop of his fingers. "We'll take off," he said. "We'll go on a trip. I gotta go to Chi sometime anyway, and we can stop at the lake. We'll hit the road, get some fresh air, a little sun and water."

"How?"

"I'll get the car. I told Nina I had to borrow it sometime to go to Chi, and I'll tell her I have to go now, the agency called me. We'll get the hell out of here."

"What'll I tell my folks?" Sonny asked.

"Nothing. Anything. Leave a note. Say you'll be back in a week, you went on a camping trip. They're at church now, aren't they?"

"Yes."

Gunner hustled Sonny back down to the car and roared off to the Burns's house. No one was there. Sonny sat down in the den, feeling dizzy, not sure what he was doing.

"Listen," he said. "No shit, Gunner, what'll I do?"

Gunner popped his fingers and pointed one at Sonny like a gun, and then, making it an order, he just said one emphatic, clear, irrefutable word, said it so there wasn't any question or confusion.

*"Pack!"*

Once in a very dark period of my own life a friend came to visit me. I was living in an especially depressing place in Greenwich Village, a small, narrow ground-floor apartment that resembled a cell, not only in size and shape, but also because of the bars on the window to discourage burglars (they discouraged me in a different way), and the blank walls and floors that I hadn't had the spirit to decorate. My friend looked around at the place and then at me, and said, "You gotta get outa here." The next day he took me to look for an apartment the two of us could share. We found a place that seemed to us palatial (two rooms, kitchen, and bath) on the top floor of a building on Bleecker Street, and I moved in with my friend, not only to a new apartment, but to a new and more productive and happier time of my life. I hate to imagine what it would have been like had he never come, had I stayed on moldering in the "cell."

I thought of all this recently as I read a marvelous quote from a play by the late Jane Chambers called *In Her Own Words*. Ms. Chambers, who was described in a review in the

*New York Times* as "not religious," wrote this: "Life is not a crapshoot. It is what we who love each other do together. And that is, in itself, sufficient."

Though Ms. Chambers may not have believed in or felt the need for a god or higher power, her philosophy, so beautifully expressed in that quote, fits my own definition of religion or spirituality as a search for the meaning of things. That meaning shines forth in "what we who love each other do together." This is a good way to think of the sort of experience we are now going to evoke and write about.

For this exercise, take crayons and paper and draw a picture of a friend or mentor or guide whom you'd like to write about, someone who helped you at a sensitive time in your life and enabled you to move on. As in all these drawings, don't worry about being an artist. Render your friend in the way you see him or her, the way you picture them in your imagination, either as person or as symbol of the special kind of goodness and help they represent.

After drawing the picture, go off in pairs and show the picture to your partner. Introduce your friend, and tell how he or she helped you on your way. (Be sure to choose someone you have not shared with before in a pair; by changing partners you get to know more people in a deeper way as you share the work of the course.)

## The Fisherman

JOHN GOULD

Grady Olsen was big, a barrel-chested, barrel-smiling man, big, about my age, from a small farm in New England. He filled the room. I met him when I was teaching creative writing at the adult education center. I was married at the time, writing cookbooks, articles, and a novel which would not be published until later, after all this was over. My wife, a former student of mine when I taught high school English, was now a student at the university.

Grady turned up in my creative writing class. He was the best of the lot, would have been the best had the lot been much better. His first story was about an army deserter returning from Canada to face arrest and I learned soon enough that the story was autobiographical. He was currently performing alternative service.

He was all outdoors. He had grown up hunting and fishing, a hard worker and a hard drinker, and now he was holding his marriage together with difficulty.

Mine was faltering, for a combination of reasons which had to do with students and teachers and truths and fictions and imaginations and realities. Nothing so prosaic as other people's bodies was involved: my wife and I were growing apart at the levels of the spirit and the psyche.

"Grady" knew this intuitively, for we did not speak of it directly. He knew I was unhappy, knew vaguely why—and as the last spring of my marriage arrived, he took me north to go fishing.

The black fly season hadn't quite hatched. We stayed in a friend's fishing-hunting camp. "Grady" arrived with a coffee can full of worms, explaining that we were there for fish, not sport. We floated on still ponds and threw back more fish than we kept.

One afternoon at dusk, he stopped at the sight of a doe near the woods. "Here, dahlin'," he called out the window, and the deer blinked beautifully, but otherwise did nothing, even after we drove on.

We came home after three days, and cooked trout for our respective spouses—mine was becoming a vegetarian—and drank more wine than we should have. Shortly afterwards the marriage was over, I was pedalling a ten-speed bicycle across the country, and "Grady" was left behind.

And I am richer for having known him. We were once talking about his times as a deserter. "You know," he said, "there's a value to the rocks in the stream." I never knew that before.

———

*Friend: A Roundabout Story*

LINDA

I was surprised to find my mother at home when I arrived from school that day. Usually, she would be working at my dad's store and I would be delivered my two little brothers to watch until she got home at dinnertime. Often I would also take care of my father in my role as oldest daughter. My brothers were four years and nine months old. My other two brothers, ten years and six years old, were on their own. I was eight—the ripe old age of eight.

Mom announced she had to go 350 miles south to the university hospital where Dad had been rushed by ambulance from our local hospital. I would be in charge of the kids as I always was. She said I could call my Aunt Margie anytime and that my older cousin Betty would come, get dinner, and stay til seven in the evening. She hoped to return in a day or two.

First she had to grocery shop—but I heard Mom say she had no money. This alarmed me. Nevertheless, she went to the local newly opened supermarket. There she was met at the door by Bill, the manager, announcing a contest. If she could beat two other ladies in unwrapping a pack and every stick of Wrigley's Spearmint gum in the pack she would win three carts full of groceries. Well, old nimble-fingers won. Dexterity was always her strength. It was our loaves-and-fishes story. Mom never felt this to be anything other than God providing. She always knew and believed He would sustain us, and this was yet another example.

I lacked that faith. The dark night came. My mother had left at five. Betty would leave at seven. I began to cry. Betty said she would stay til ten o'clock. She cancelled her plans and helped me put the kids to bed. I was so grateful.

At ten Betty left. I crawled into my parents' bed—a privileged place to sleep, but that night strangely empty of comfort. My four-year-old's fear of bears in the woods returned. Our door was unlocked as always. No one would hear us scream if burglars came—the houses were so isolated in the country.

I heard the dark speaking. This would be the very night a chicken hawk would attack our baby chickens. Our rabbits would probably be killed by rats. I imagined what it would feel like to be a chicken or rabbit in those circumstances. I had heard that the guy down the road who had killed his daughter was out of prison. I wondered if he knew we were alone. I got under the bed. I wondered if I should get the other kids under the bed too, but I knew if I woke them and we were all under one bed they would fight, and the noise would alert the burglars and murderers to where we were. Abandoned and alone, I felt the lack of God.

Morning came. I was ecstatic to see the light of day. I heard my brothers fighting. I knew they were awake. My sweet baby brother clung to me when I went to him. I peeked out the window. The rabbits were alive. The chickens were peeping. I was relieved beyond belief to see light and life.

I gave the kids breakfast. My older brother took the two little boys to our one-room school. My mother had thought that would be a good day for Pat, who was four years old, to visit school (he was still too young to go). The boys cooperated, as children do when they sense the fragility of their environment.

The school was having its only yearly trip that afternoon. The John Deere tractor show was in town. John Deere brought their latest farm equipment to our town in an attempt to sell to the farmers and the future farmers, those of us in school. Mom thought I shouldn't miss this exciting event, so my Aunt Margie would come at noon, pick up my baby brother Bob, and drop me off at school. I had stayed home from school that morning to care for Bob.

I did not want to go to school. I did not want to give this sweet baby over to my Aunt Margie. I knew she considered us such a bother. She was always having to pick up the pieces in our house, and she resented it. She made us stay outside unless it was pouring rain. She came. I packed Bobby up to go to her house. I got in the car and held Bobby in my lap until we got to school. He began wailing and screaming when I tried to get out of the car and put him down. He clung to me like glue. Aunt Margie pried him loose from me. I was left with the ring of his despairing screams in my ears. I walked holding my own tears in.

I reached the school door and walked in. I felt the excitement in the room about the coming trip but I did not feel part of it. It was all something I observed but did not feel at all connected to. All I could hear and think about was Bobby.

I walked quietly to my desk and sat down. I put my head down and my arms around my head. I sobbed quietly, unaware of anything but the sorrow in my heart. Bobby's screams still rang in my ears.

Then I felt a gentle touch on my shoulder. I peeked up to

see my teacher looking at me with loving concern. She asked me what was wrong. I told her I didn't know.

Somehow that was it. That's as much profile as I can give of Bonnie Wheelock, my third-grade teacher. She didn't demand I verbalize what I couldn't, but she communicated by her touch and look that she *knew* I was despairing. That was one of the few times in my life I felt anyone knew the grief and anger and despair I felt living in my house. And just that recognition of my inner reality made me feel like I was loved.

Later that summer I was walking somewhere. Bonnie offered me a ride. She said, "Remember that day you cried in school? I always wondered what was wrong." I still couldn't verbalize. I got out of her car soon after, and ran from the memory. I don't think Bonnie ever knew how much it meant to me that she asked.

----

### Robbie Kreitentott

ALAN BODNAR

The house where I grew up as an only child was wedged between two others; one the residence of two elderly couples, the other the home of my recently married and still childless aunt and uncle. The rest of the triangular block was given over to public buildings—the city hall with offices upstairs and a jail on the first floor, and the board of health building adjacent to our back yard. Across the street from our front door was a dance hall with a telephone booth that we, being without such amenities, used to communicate with others. All of this is my way of saying that there were no children in the neighborhood with whom I could play.

One of the best things about school was the chance to be with other children, and one of them, Robert Kreitentott, soon became my best friend. Robbie lived up the hill in a neighborhood about a mile away from my house. Every day after school we would take turns visiting each other, and we played together all day on Saturdays. During the time of year when it got dark around six o'clock, our parents told us to start for home when we saw the street lights go on. Neither of us had wristwatches, and even if we had they probably wouldn't have survived our adventures.

Robbie was a rugged, handsome boy with bright blue eyes and his hair cut in the fashionable flattop style. I was of slighter build, but I persuaded my mother to let me get a flattop, too. Robbie and I competed to see who could comb his top the flattest and I think he won easily. Maybe he had an unfair advantage because his head was so square. Oh, how I longed to be square and angular like Bobby! Even his name, Robert Kreitentott, was all points, angles and corners while I was stuck with the hopelessly round Alan. Robbie had a brother twenty years older than us who was in the Air Force, and I remember how the two of us formed a club called the Blue Angels. We'd pretend to be jet fighters and fly through the marshlands and gritty factory precincts of our small town. Once, when we were nine, Robbie and I were chasing pigeons on the steps of the city hall and climbing to the head of a stone lion guarding the portals of justice. Bobby jumped to the ground, landed on his feet and urged me to follow. My ill-fated attempt at being a stunt man, however, landed me in the hospital for a week with a concussion.

Maybe something got shaken up in my brain, because I began to surpass my friend in our schoolwork. When we were in the eighth grade and interested in the same girls, our competition took on a new dimension. At times I felt my main role was to carry the extra books Robbie couldn't handle after having three girls at once ask him to carry their books home from school. For seven years now, fate had been leading us to a decisive confrontation. It came in the form of the race for eighth-grade class president: Bobby and I ran against each other. When the ballots had all been counted, he had won by a single vote, but it happened because I had voted for him, as he himself had. It was one of my first lessons in the importance of self-confidence. Other lessons would follow, and Robbie Kreitentott was often the teacher. We went to different high schools and different colleges. He became the all-state football player and I the valedictorian of my graduating class. We'd get together on holidays and over summer vacation, usually to play basketball or tennis and, in those sports, we'd usually break even. I was the best man at Robbie's wedding—he married first. A year or so after my own wedding, Robbie, while on a business trip to Boston, visited me and my wife. He and his wife were on the verge of divorcing, but he seemed undaunted. There he sat in all his rugged splendor, discussing philosophy and morality.

I saw him one more time. My wife and I were visiting Washington, D.C., and he met us on his lunch hour to give us a tour of the capital. He had remarried and seemed to be doing well. There were no hints of the sadness that I knew must be there after an earlier visit I had had with his first wife and two little girls. Though we've lost track of each other, the memories of our friendship remain an important part of my childhood. Thanks to Robbie, my own self-picture is a little more angular, but I also know that there's nothing wrong with being round.

———

## Clever Writing

ANONYMOUS

I have always been a shy, indecisive person, and when the time came for me to go to college, I felt particularly timid. So instead of applying to college as my friends were, I decided to work full-time after graduation. I would only work for a year, and the delay, I thought, would give me the money and courage I needed. Two weeks after graduation, I became an actuarial clerk for a large insurance company in Boston. At first I loved working in the city and earning money, but after a while the boredom overwhelmed me. I still felt terribly confused about what to do, and college still felt too threatening. So I stayed at work, getting promotions, but never feeling very satisfied.

At that time in my life, I read biographies whenever I felt indecisive or confused. I always figured that I would somehow get the answers I needed by reading about someone else's life. One day I read Moss Hart's autobiography, *Act One*. I couldn't believe the connection I felt. Like me, he came from an eccentric family with little money. He too had a boring job when he was my age. And he didn't go to college. He got out of his rut by writing humorous plays about his family. That was the answer, I decided. I would start writing funny pieces to cope with boredom. Before I started writing, though, I read as much humor as I could. I grew obsessed with humorists' lives and work. All this gave me instant relief from the emptiness I felt in my own life.

A few years later, I decided to take a writing class to test my interest in humorous writing. I signed up for a class called "The Craft of Writing." My teacher was a soft-spoken, gray-haired woman in her sixties. She was not what I expected. She was gentle, and talked about how we would get to know each other well. We would write about what mattered to us. It would be a way of discovering ourselves. I had never thought of writing this way. To me, writing had always been a performance, a way for someone else to discover me. Our first assignment was to write a profile of someone we knew and I decided to describe my wild, annoying roommate. I made sure I was clever. When I finished I thought I had done a good job. I confidently handed in the paper.

Two weeks later I got the paper back. I read the comments. My teacher said it was boring. I was crushed. How could something clever be boring? I was so upset that I decided to talk to the teacher about it. She told me that she had read it and kept comparing it to the in-class pieces I had written. They were more real and moving, she said. I couldn't understand this, because they were often about childhood memories, many of them sad. I wanted to write funny pieces because I thought no one would be interested in the truth. But my teacher kept telling me I needed to write in a real way. I had never heard this before. I decided to stop being clever. It was the first time that anyone was interested in my real life. I felt I had been pushed in the right direction.

--------

## The Entertainer

POLLY BATES

I had my first migraine when I was three years old. I don't remember it, but my mother tells me we were at a family party at a friend's house when I suddenly rushed into the house clutching my head and screaming. The next few years were an endless round of medications that didn't work and medical tests that severely tried my patience. Looking back, I can see that the migraines colored my childhood. They struck out of the blue, incapacitating me for hours or days. Every time something exciting was about to happen, it seemed, I got sick. At high points that I had looked forward to for weeks, such as my ninth birthday party and my older brother's college graduation, I ended up in bed in a darkened room trying not to throw up. I was sick on so many car trips that one of my brothers, in exasperation, declared I should wear a sign around my neck saying "ten-feet clearance." That certainly didn't make me feel better.

A migraine isn't one pain, but rather a multitude of symptoms. Mine always concentrated in the right part of my forehead above my eye, with a dull relentless throbbing that sent waves of nausea over the rest of me. All of my senses would be intensified so that the slightest light, noise, or smell would bang on my nerves. If I turned my head, the pain in my forehead would singe the right side of my face. I learned that only one position would minimize my discomfort: curled in bed on my right side, I would firmly wrap the pillow around the lower part of my face, leaving just my left eye peering out. I sometimes had to lie like this for hours, perfectly still, with the fading afternoon light filtering through the curtains.

Far off, I could hear the sounds of the household: muffled voices, the *tv*, pans clattering in the kitchen. It felt so unnatural to be in bed at that hour. Normally, I enjoyed puttering around in my room—it was a cozy haven from the rest of the family—but when I had a migraine it became suffocating. I hated being closed off from the world; I hated losing all those precious daytime hours. Lying in bed, I often felt life was moving on without me—that I was missing out on vital moments I would never be able to recapture. Once well again and back on my feet, I would feel a lingering sadness, as though I had been sent away on a long journey and, now returning, found myself a step out of sync with everyone else.

Sleep during a migraine was usually impossible. Instead, I tried to distance myself from the pain by focusing my thoughts on some faraway subject. This wasn't always easy to do, and often, overwhelmed with frustration and sick of the discomfort, I broke down in tears, bringing my mother rushing in to look on helplessly. She tried reading my favorite books to me but I couldn't concentrate on the words—it only made my head worse. At these moments, it seemed as if I would never feel normal again.

What finally saved me was my younger brother. When I was ten, Nicholas was eight and just starting to suffer the ill effects in school of his then-undiagnosed dyslexia. He couldn't read, compensated by misbehaving, and was generally unpopular with students and teachers alike. His once ebullient nature had dampened into a resigned sense of failure, and he spent a lot of time watching *tv* by himself.

When I was ill, though, he started coming in to visit me. Normally hyperactive and boisterous, he would carefully restrain himself, quietly closing the door and tiptoeing in. With reading not an option, Nicholas entertained me with a vast array of tricks: skits, singing and dancing, making up funny words and definitions. Those afternoons became as much a creative outlet for him as a distraction for me. One time when my head was especially bad, I remember he did a lengthy take-off of Walter Cronkite's newscast, complete with graphics—drawings he held up over his shoulder. I thought it was hilarious, and it swiftly chased away the headache.

Alienated from his old circle of friends, Nicholas perhaps felt honored to be welcome in his older sister's room. I in turn felt enormous gratitude that he would while away his afternoons and evenings with me, a social leper of sorts. It got so whenever I had a migraine, Nick would eagerly trot into my room with a new set of jokes. We also started talking about serious things, too, our parents, school. For the first time it occurred to me that my baby brother was someone I could like. I came to rely on him.

Gradually, as I got older, my migraines became less frequent. I spent less time in bed, and more time with my friends. But as much as everything else over the years has changed, my close friendship with my brother has stayed the same, and I trace it back to those lonely, late-afternoon hours, when only he could keep me company.

———

## A Healing Path

NANCY

Our therapy group for women adult children of alcoholics had been meeting for over four months now. Five of us climbed the oak staircase each week to a second-floor apartment in an old frame house on a tree-lined street. The flat belonged to Laura, one of our group leaders, an earth-mother type of woman in her thirties. Jane was the other one, a deceptively reserved little person who, behind her slightly owlish glasses and mild manner, was a powerhouse of sensitive skill and uncanny insight.

We had come there first in September, a motley crew of five guarded, tense, wounded individuals, who were there out of desperate pain and need, but who were all very careful about how much we would risk reaching out or letting others in. I personally held tightly to what had been my central and most effective survival defense for over fifty years: my ability to analyze, verbalize, intellectualize *ad infinitum*—everything but to open up and feel out loud with others, to accept the solace of sharing and support from the heart.

That particular evening in a snowy, frigid February, after the usual "check-in" period of sharing and processing whatever we wished from the week past, our leaders told us gently but firmly that the agenda was to do some work at getting in touch with our respective inner "lost children"—our own "little girls."

To establish a relaxing atmosphere, pillows had been tossed comfortably about on the floor of the small living room, around which we usually sat on several chairs and a sofa. Jane and Laura invited us to get on the floor among the pillows, lie down, or just relax in any way we wished, and to listen while Jane read aloud a children's story to us. Anne, a tall, dark-haired mother closest in age to me, stretched out immediately in delighted anticipation, chuckling and obviously enjoying letting go into her little-girl self. Martha and Dorine, two very different but very courageous young women, joked around a bit nervously and took a while getting settled, but they, too, finally quieted and leaned easily against pillows each had propped up, one against a chair and the other against the sofa. Even Wendy, the shyest of us all, dropped to the rug against the tall bookcase and took an attitude of repose, her long hair partially hiding her wide eyes. But I—I alone remained on the sofa, cutting myself off, sitting upright, legs and arms crossed, and announced that I couldn't get onto the floor because of my back problem.

Well, there was some truth to it, but if that had been all, it wouldn't have stopped me. I had come there that night in a foul mood, tense, angry, tight in the throat. Things in my life, particularly its central relationships, had been falling apart that week. I was warding off the pain and fear for all I was worth, and the form this took was hostility toward the group, not as individuals, but as a commitment that had forced me out on a night when all I wanted was to retreat into my inner escape hole and hide.

So I sat stiff-backed on the sofa exactly like the stereotypical "schoolteacher" image I hated, and put up a mighty wall against the playful mood of the others, against the loving atmosphere, and against the warm story Jane began to read to us in her gentle, mothering voice.

When she finally finished and the spell wound down, she asked that each of us get quiet for a few minutes and then begin to write a letter to her own "little girl" within—her lost inner child. Gradually I was conscious of the others rustling paper, murmuring, shifting position, and then settling down, pens scratching.

I sat, furious, bewildered, disdainful, rebellious—and terrified. My mind worked madly to come to my defense. Finally, a last ditch cry of "I'll fix them" choking within me, I picked up my pen and began to write a sentence which was going to read: "Dear Nancy—I can't do this. Sorry." Period.

Instead, what came from my pen—from some power deep beyond my understanding—were the words, "Dear Hase"— the soft German term that was my father's childhood pet name for me, his "little rabbit." And as though a secret key had turned in an old stiff lock, the words continued to pour out, an intense, gentle, halting communication of love and protectiveness.

But when the writing was done, Jane said quietly that we'd now read our letter aloud. My rage and panic rose hot in my mouth again, though mixed now with new, deeper, more turbulent feelings. Unfair—a trick! But two of the others read first, and my defenses weakened as I felt moved by their voices and words. At last I girded myself and began to read the strange and surprising words on my own page, determined to just get through it quickly, so I could shut down again—before it was too late—before I was too far from shore.

But as I reached the last few lines, hearing my own parenting voice talking to the child whom I suddenly felt palpably was really in there, my voice broke. For the first time since the group began—really for the first time ever—the old, long-hoarded tears came, and then the sobs. I felt as though I were suddenly adrift and sinking in a vast ocean of memory, loss, and grief.

Then—just as I was drowning—I felt Dorine's small but amazingly strong hand reach from the floor and clasp one of my own. Martha's long, artistic fingers found and firmly enclosed the other one. Looking up through the salt blur, I saw not only their faces but those of Anne and Wendy and Jane and Laura, all there with me, eyes full of silent comprehension and love. The waters seemed literally to roll back on either side. A healing path stretched suddenly before me, and I knew the meaning of spiritual communion.

# 8 Fourth Exercise: A Road Map of Your Spiritual Journey

How did you get where you are?

Sometimes we stop to ask the question and are baffled and overwhelmed. The idea of looking back on our life journey to write about it seems too formidable, too complicated. So much has happened! How can we ever sort it out, make sense of it? How can we even think of writing about it if we can't "see" it?

Drawing a "road map" of our life enables us to do just that: see the "picture" of our journey. Just as we could write different kinds of autobiographies—romantic, economic, professional, or educational—so we could also draw different kinds of maps that showed how we got to the point we have reached in those categories (partnership, bank account, job, or college degree). To draw a map of our spiritual journey is to look for the experiences and changes, the turning points, triumphs and crashes, dark nights and mountain peaks we each have traversed to become the kind of person we are (which is, among other things, a person who at this point in their life wants to write a spiritual autobiography).

The map we draw may, of course, include some points of all the different kinds of biography described above (such milestones as college graduation, parenthood, move to a new city or a new job) but may also include more interior experience—

the arid times that seem like wastelands, or the flowering of creativity. We are all pilgrims whose progress is marked by sloughs of despond as well as what Churchill called "the broad uplands" of human experience.

We have all known thunderstorms and lightning, sunshine and rainbows, earthquakes of doubt or illness, and made ascents to peaks of understanding and accomplishment. Symbolic pictures of life experience might include all those images as well as a host of others, such as bridges burned, bursts of sunlight, forks in the road, dangerous curves, peaceful valleys, flooding rivers, placid lakes, personal or professional battlefields, spires of ambition, hearts in love.

Using a big sheet of paper and lots of crayons, take thirty to forty-five minutes to draw the road map of your own journey. Think about it first, perhaps making a few notes of what you want to include. Give it whatever shape or form feels right for you. Some people start with a line or road that goes from left to right and then right to left across the page. Some start from the center and go outward in a circle; others move up and down the paper like a fever chart or graph of change, charting the ups and downs of life. There is no right or wrong way to do it, only what feels natural for you, the way your own life seems to "lay out."

After drawing your road map, pair up with another person and take ten minutes to describe it to him or her, answering questions they may have about it, then switch and hear about theirs for an equal amount of time. You will inevitably learn more about your journey as you describe it to your partner— and also as you look at and hear about theirs.

When you finish your road map, you have an outline, a reference point, or a starting place for writing your spiritual autobiography. In the eight-week course, this means the writing of an eight-to-ten-page paper that will be read in class. In a day-long or weekend workshop or retreat, this means that when you leave you have a "map" that will serve as inspiration and supply a "plot" for whatever kind of spiritual autobiography you wish to write, of whatever length or form you wish it to take (anything from a few pages to a book!). Once you have written your spiritual autobiography, you may wish to continue writing a "spiritual journal," keeping track of the deeper experience of your ongoing inner and outer travels. You may at some point want to look back at the journal and use it as raw material for further writing, to be developed as essays or stories, or used as inspiration for poetry or personal meditations or prayers.

Many people tape or tack their road map to the wall of their study or above their desk, or keep it handy for reference as they continue to write. You can return to any of the points shown on it for material, using it like a mine of rich ore, a treasure trove of experience.

After the drawing and sharing of the road map, I like to distribute a quote from Henri Nouwen, the Dutch theologian and priest whose writing about spirituality gives me continuing insight as well as inspiration. The quote is from his book *Reaching Out*, which Rev. Carl Scovel loaned me early in my own journey. The question Father Nouwen poses can be asked of anyone, regardless of religion or lack of any formal religious belief. When I read and distribute it, I emphasize that I don't know the answer to the question he raises (in fact I change my mind about it from time to time), but that it helps me look at my experience in a deeper and more creative way. It is a pertinent and provocative idea to keep in mind as you begin to write your spiritual autobiography, or in fact whenever you try to understand your life from a spiritual vantage point. This is what Father Nouwen wrote:

> What if the events of our history are molding us as a sculptor molds his clay, and if it is only in a careful obedience to these molding hands that we can discover our real vocation and become mature people? What if all the unexpected interruptions are in fact invitations to give up old-fashioned and out-moded styles of living and are opening up new unexplored areas of experience? And finally: What if our history does not prove to be a blind impersonal sequence of events over which we have no control,

but rather reveals to us a guiding hand pointing to a personal encounter in which all our hopes and aspirations will reach their fulfillment?

Then our life would indeed be different, because then fate becomes opportunity, wounds a warning, and paralysis an invitation to search for deeper sources of vitality.

# 9 Spiritual Autobiographies of a Class

This is the story of a class I led in spiritual autobiography, and more importantly, it is an introduction to the participants' stories, the papers they wrote as part of the course. We gathered in the library on the first floor of the Boston Center for Adult Education, an old mansion on Commonwealth Avenue near the Public Garden in downtown Boston. The place has a wonderful ambience of warmth and grace. The high ceilings, the wide stairway, and even the chandeliers in the ballroom (where I took a t'ai chi class) suggest not stuffy grandeur but an old world, Bostonian charm. Its character manifests not Brahmin exclusivity (in which "the Cabots speak only to Lowells, and the Lowells speak only to God"), but a respect for education as exploration, in the way Emerson and his circle would have seen it.

I first went to the Boston Center for a poetry reading in a snowstorm in the winter of 1974, and later returned to take courses there in t'ai chi, hatha yoga, and French cooking (sampling the best of East and West). I have always enjoyed this dark-wooded, nineteenth-century setting for the casual, friendly coming together of people from different backgrounds interested in learning more about all kinds of things, not for grades or credits but rather to enhance the experience of their own lives. It is one of the places that feels like home to me, and the first place I thought of when I decided to offer the course in spiritual autobiography "out in the world" after taking it in my own church.

This is how I described the course for the catalog: "Whether or not you're formally 'religious,' you've probably sensed a power beyond yourself that influences and gives greater meaning to your life. The search to understand that power is one of the favorite themes of great literature as expressed by Homer, T. S. Eliot, Thomas Merton, and the Bible. Through discussion, writing exercises, drawing, and reading, we will explore the way in which we have personally experienced that power in our lives, and we'll work toward producing an eight-to-ten-page spiritual autobiography. The accounts of other people's experiences as they journeyed through Zen, Judaism, Christianity, and nature will also be considered."

That was the promise that brought fourteen people together the first Monday night of November 1988, and I would say that this promise was fulfilled in spirit (more fully than I would have imagined) if not all the details. I had first led the course there the previous year, and found that the readings I had assigned in other people's journeys did not elicit as much discussion or interest as I had hoped, so when time became short, I neglected those outside readings in favor of spending all the time on the work of the class.

This has been my experience in the spiritual autobiography courses at King's Chapel, as well. Though we read selections from a variety of spiritual works from Saint Augustine to Thomas Merton, nothing seemed to really click as a creative stimulus for this particular kind of class. In writing spiritual autobiography, the work being done by you and your fellow students is so immediate and of so much personal interest (and having just been written, fresher than any published work!), that it is of little value to include the writing of "outsiders," no matter how brilliant or classic it may be.

Certainly the papers evoked by the exercises on childhood, adolescence, and a friend on the journey were fascinating, yet I found myself feeling nervous and apprehensive on the first night people would read their full spiritual autobiography. I had come to feel I knew the class members well enough to be anxious for all of them to "succeed" (as if there were any way to "fail" in such an enterprise), in the sense of producing an autobiography that would be meaningful to them, and then by definition to the others.

JANA     The first person to read was "Jana," the pen name of a woman who describes herself as a "single grandmother on last third of this lifetime (expecting others), and currently consumed by the excitement, wonder, and mystery of self-discovery, the challenge of entrepreneurship, the exhaustion of single parenting, the sadness of an aging parent, and the indescribable joy of grandchildren." As she took a deep breath before reading, I took one myself, and listened to her paper.

*Out of the Monastery of the World*

During the past seven years, I have believed that I was on a spiritual journey in search of the self I lost, many years ago, when I chose to live a life defined by others. My story is about the realization of that loss and the mission I have had to redefine my own life.

I had a crisis of faith when I was twenty-three years old. I didn't know that at the time, of course. Only later was I able to understand what I was experiencing that night, very late, sitting alone in the kitchen of my new home. I should have been very happy. Instead a cold, empty, free-floating anxiety gripped me because I was not able to feel any connection with God any longer. Suddenly, I was frightened and pained, very, very pained. Was I an atheist? The term sent shivers down my spine. Me? My god. How could that possibly happen to me? The anxiety, the loss, the embarrassment of this strange state of being left me desolate, not knowing where to turn.

William Blake says, "Self-evident truth is one thing and Truth the result of reasoning is another Thing. Rational truth is not the truth of Christ, but of Pilate." My discomfort that night, I suppose, was the loss I felt of things self-evident, and my new uncomfortable association with Pilate, which I would carry on for the next twenty years.

The process leading to my disbelief had been going on for

a number of years. In retrospect, the doubt I had been experiencing seemed to coincide with a decision I had made not to follow my own instincts, desires, and needs with regard to a major life decision. Instead, I succumbed to my mother's wishes. As I write this, it is the first time I have ever connected the two events.

Romantic expectations not realized at that age can be devastating, and when the boy I had planned to marry seemed to have some doubts about our relationship, I rejected him, in fear that he would reject me. In actuality, our relationship was superficial at best (he had been stationed overseas a good deal of the time we had known each other), and so there was really no depth to the relationship, but he had met my romantic ideal at the time, and he had the proper family background.

With this loss of love, my assumptive world collapsed around me for the first time. I floundered. I didn't know quite what to do or where to turn. And even though one of the vice presidents of the company I worked at suggested I be sent to classes in the evening in connection with my work, I was neither excited nor interested. I felt only my injury.

Shortly thereafter, in an effort to move on with my life, I decided to move to Washington, D.C. with a friend. Politics had always been a major interest during my school years. (In my senior year, I was fascinated and challenged by my government class, and my teacher demonstrated his confidence in me when he publicly declared to the entire class that I was the only one capable of getting an A on a major exam.)

They needed secretaries in the Navy Department in Washington and I applied, was accepted, purchased my suitcases, and was all set to leave, a bit frightened, but very, very excited. Disappointingly, however, my friend changed her plans, which then changed mine. Without her support and company, I was not able to withstand my mother's challenge, which came when I was very close to leaving and she saw that I was serious about going. The image of my leaving home without her approval so frightened me that I became paralyzed and immediately changed my plans.

I was nineteen years old, and it was at this point that I began to live two different lives. Mistakenly feeling no other options open to me, I rebounded into a relationship, boarding the marriage train two years later and reluctantly closing one door in my life—certain testimony to that sage wisdom that youth is wasted on the young.

My guardian angel, however, looking out for my best interests in spite of me, opened up another door when he brought me to a Boston publishing house, as a secretary. I had entered a new world, one I had no prior knowledge of, and I was fascinated as I experienced Brahmin Boston for the first time. I was captivated by the atmosphere, and discovered an important new part of myself in this new world of books. A new life of the mind opened up to me. I had found my own personal magic carpet.

I was married when I was twenty-one. Although the next seven years of my life were naturally filled with the discovery and thrill of new beginnings, ideas, and places, and the excitement and idealism of youth, they were also filled with pervasive feelings of regret about my marriage and the pain of enduring three pregnancies, all of which ended in stillbirths. In doing my life map, the only way I could think of describing the pain of those losses was with black tears, lots and lots of black tears.

So many sad memories from that time come to my mind. The most traumatic is one of my leaving a world famous infertility clinic one early evening after I had been told by my young and supposedly brilliant doctor (in what I remember was probably a rather too matter-of-fact manner) that the baby I was carrying was dead. I was utterly devastated, stunned, and disbelieving; the shock paralyzed me, while the doctor and his nurse seemed to go about their business as if nothing had happened. Managing to barely hold myself together until I was alone outside in the night, and looking up at the sky, I screamed out in total rage at God, "I hate you, I hate you." I couldn't believe it was happening to me, again.

There were other black tears on my life map for that period in time. Tears for Jack Kennedy, killed on that monumentally painful day in November 1963, when I felt like something inside me had been killed—that special something that each of us believes we have and saw in him. The sadness I felt at his sudden death overwhelmed me for days, and I have no doubt that the hope and enthusiasm of a whole generation was ravaged on that day. I was twenty-seven years old.

About this time, and for the first time, I began to be concerned about the amount of reading I was doing. It was a great deal, and I wondered about the dangers of living too much in one's head. But fortunately, my concerns were forgotten as I entered the most contented period of my life, the years between 1965 and 1979.

In December 1965, all the pain of loss disappeared when we brought our adopted son home. It was the happiest day of my life up to that moment, and I believed, finally, without a doubt, that the suffering I had endured had meaning and purpose. In May 1967, we picked up our beautiful baby girl.

In 1968 I became active in the League of Women Voters, finally finding a satisfying outlet for my interests in politics and government, as well as wonderful new friends. I had missed the camaraderie I had had in high school, and rediscovered it again in a far more satisfying and mature way in a group of bright active women concerned with making a difference.

In 1970 we moved into what I thought was a dream house, lovelier than any I had expected to own. Feminism was a powerful new force during that time, and my continued interest in the League provided me with an opportunity to meet and work with interesting women in the community. It was during this time that we often got together at my home to do committee work and that I began to experience other women in a real way, not as role-playing happy little homemakers.

The early seventies were filled with discoveries for me: that I was not alone in an unhappy marriage was an important one. I was surprised and relieved to learn that I was not nearly as foolish as I had felt all those years, and that other women had also succumbed to social pressures to marry.

I can actually make the claim that a book changed my life

at this time. It was entitled *You Are Not the Target*. I don't remember the author. But it seemed to shout at me as I passed it on the library shelf. It contained new information for me about the psychology of human behavior and explanations about things that had always confounded me. The sudden realization that other people weren't perfect either, and had the same doubts and insecurities as I did was a healing experience. I was inspired by the book and made the decision to learn everything I could about psychological health and growth.

Almost simultaneously with the reading of the book, I attended an introductory workshop about heightened states of consciousness. I began to have experiences which were almost euphoric. When I had the first experience, it was so glorious that it suddenly occurred to me that the feeling I was having and the term "born again" might have some connection. Although I never thought of my experience as a religious one (since my focus was always on *psychological* health), when I came upon William James's description of the "twice-born" man years later, I strongly identified with it.

My first and last experience with a psychiatrist occurred during those years, prompted by an anguished concern about my marriage. The doctor lifted my sadness immediately with a healing lecture about the dangers of martyrdom, which regretfully was the only feminine model I had seen growing up. Leaving his office, my spirits soared, and I believed that I in fact did have choices, as long as I could accept the ramifications. I remained committed to my marriage, the guilt I had been carrying around disappeared, and I experienced an enormous sense of well-being.

These years passed with more happiness than sadness in a predictable fashion until, one day, there began a series of events which I found somewhat astonishing when I connected them. They began one night while I was on my way home. The commuter train I was on, leaving North Station, refused to go forward, and finding myself standing next to a man I knew (his name was Tom) and his wife, I began to talk with him about the law firm I was working at. Tom had an employment agency and I had occasion to call him when we needed secretaries.

Overhearing our conversation, a stranger standing next to me suddenly joined in, probably settling into the anticipation of a long wait. He was an attorney, so found the conversation Tom and I were having of some interest. He was a tall man, dark-haired, ordinarily attractive, and generally unremarkable in appearance. As a conversationalist, however, he was thoroughly engaging, so I managed to forget Tom and his wife completely. I asked him his name as he was leaving the train. He replied, "After what I've told you, I'm certainly not going to tell you my name." I can still feel the smile his words brought to my lips when he left. I remember feeling that something special had happened between us, not of a romantic nature, but something more simple and basic.

That summer, the summer of 1979, a second book came into my life and, again, I was profoundly affected by it. It was a spiritual biography of Werner Erhard by a philosophy professor named W. W. Bartley III. It was the amazing story of the founder of Est, and in the course of reading it something happened to me. I had a sense of things coming together. One day while meditating, I began to experience God in the way I had as a child, and a sense of grace came over me and seemed to enter my life again. It was miraculous and was later explained to me in this way: when I lost that connection with God as a young woman, what I really lost was my childlike concept of God, and later through meditation I was able to reexperience God (the voice of the silence) as part of myself. Apparently this was not unusual, and many people have reexperienced God in this way.

Well, there I was in this new wondrous state of being again, when suddenly the earthquake struck my marriage and I had an explosive argument with my husband. A book entitled *The Intimate Enemy* states, "The danger of a nuclear explosion hovers over every nonfighting marriage." One night, when we were out with friends—I was in an exceptionally good mood—my husband said something provocative and unusually callous and, in a flash, my exceptional mood was transformed into the most intense cold anger that I had ever experienced. An astonishing explosion of immense magnitude erupted between us. It was as if someone had poured invisible gasoline around us and our words became matches.

Later that night, when it was over and I was alone with my thoughts, I felt appalled at my marriage and at our behavior, which suddenly revealed to me the intense anger just underneath the surface of our lives. As I went to bed that night I realized that I would not remain married to my husband for the rest of my life.

The fear that knowledge brought me on that fateful evening (as if a compelling new force had entered my life) was bearable only because of my reawakened faith in God. In retrospect, I've often wondered if the pressure I was feeling was spiritual, since it was so compelling.

Not long after my return to work that fall, I received a call from Tom (my friend on the train) offering me a position with his small company, selling and managing part of his operation. Over lunch, he explained that the reason for his offer was my conversation with the stranger on the train, which he and his wife had overheard and apparently enjoyed as much as we. His wife had suggested that I was either quite mad or quite talented conversationally, so he felt I would make a dynamic representative for his company. I was delighted, of course, but quite taken aback when he gave me the reason for his offer. How curious, I thought. Coincidence, of course.

When I gave notice to the managing partner of the law firm I worked at, I told him that I did so regretfully, but that the nature of my work was so mundane that I had no choice. What followed was one extraordinary event after another. First, he asked me what work I had done besides my current job. When I told him about my background, he threw a three- or four-page job description across his desk and asked if I thought I could handle it. The position was a unique and fascinating one. I was totally flabbergasted. I told him that of course I could handle it, whereupon he told me that the only hurdle that had to be overcome was an interview with the

managing trustee. Because I would finally have an opportunity to be doing challenging and interesting work, I was
very impatient about the interview, which was delayed because the new managing trustee was away.

It was February, and I was sitting at my desk, pondering
my anxiety over wanting the position so badly, when the
stranger from the train walked by. I was taken aback. He
didn't see me and went into our conference room. Something
compelled me to ask someone the date, which in fact turned
out to be the anniversary of our meeting on the train. I sat
back. Suddenly all my anxiety left and I knew the position
was mine. Wasn't his presence proof enough? I was right.

I was divorced the following year.

When she finished, I felt a whole new apprehension. I was
fearful that the others would be intimidated by such a wonderful piece, such a marvelous story, and would somehow feel
diminished.

I need not have worried. Each had a different tale to tell,
fresh and in no way comparable to the others, and each told it
with unique style and insight. Each paper, like each person,
was an extraordinary universe all its own.

————

STEVEN
JAY
KLARER

Steve Klarer is a tall, bearded man alternately intense and
casual, who has an acupuncture and body work practice in
Boston's Back Bay. He is "a survivor of child abuse and works
with survivors of child abuse" in his practice. He has studied
Chinese language and culture since 1962 and for thirteen years
was a monk in the tradition of Chinese Buddhism. He said
over coffee the other day that he was an "Air Force brat," and
has lived "all over," settling in Boston in 1983 because it reminded him of Europe more than any other American city.

*Finding*
*My Name*

"This is a play about memory and desire, about words and
the sounds we live in. Think of it. . . . names make us known
to family and to strangers. . . . Names tell us about a life
and the memory of that life. . . . Here now they are as easily

erased as the markings on tissue paper. . . . Now the page . . . is clean of names that belong here, that have a right to be here. . . . Our memories are full of names. Names are as natural as trees, birds, breathing. They are the right of a person, but there are those who believe they can take the people and their names away, and this must not happen. Names must never, never be stolen again."
—Laurence Thornton, *Imagining Argentina*

My name is Steven Jay Klarer. It hasn't always been that, although it is the name my parents chose when I was born. Besides, it's not the only name they gave me; there was, of course, the ritual patronymic Shmuel ben-David by which I would always be known in the synagogue.

My parents are not the only ones to have given me names. At first, I suppose, they used baby names, silly names and terms of endearment that had no history or meaning beyond the cooings and gurglings of the moment. They were probably just like the names that mothers all over the world have always used for their babies, names that just say "baby." As I became a toddler and a little boy, the usual variants of my name, in both English and Yiddish, were used.

Our street ended at the edge of the Bronx Park Zoo. I would often go there with my slightly older cousins on the "free days" when our parents would let us go, when it would not cost us anything. The first thing we saw as we went into the zoo was a pond with ducks and geese. I thought it remarkable that two such similar animals should have different names. Clearly they were not the same but, to my eye, the difference was mostly one of size. I watched and learned the differences and was delighted to be able to tell at a glance a duck and a goose. Further into the zoo were all sorts of creatures with not only wonderful shapes, colors, noises, and smells, but also with deliciously weird and magnificent names.

In the ape house I learned the distinctions among orangutans, chimps, and gorillas. I could soon tell the difference between an African and an Indian elephant, as well as that between dromedary and Bactrian camels. Most of all, I remember the pen with the llamas and alpacas. I was so proud of my ability to tell them apart, of my knowledge that the alpaca coat I wore in the winter came from this kind of creature, and of my knowledge that, even though they didn't have humps, these guys were a kind of camel and like camels could and would spit.

Things changed, and we left that world of New York which looked so fondly back to the Eastern European *shtetls* even as it looked to the American suburbs. We lived in several other states and countries. I moved through grade school, high school, and started university. After one year I decided to take a year off and work, in order to be able to go to school in France. During this time I began to study both French and Chinese.

In 1964 I enrolled in the National School of Oriental Languages at the University of Paris. Among my many foreign and French friends was a man named Alyosha Huang-sung. The world was so different then, and we were so young. It is strange to talk like this when I'm only forty-four, like an old man remembering a vanished time. But it's true, isn't it? The world we shared as students is gone. In Paris in the early sixties there was only one university, located as it had been for a hundred years on the left bank of the river. The new universities with artificial campuses were just about to be built and the unrest that would erupt in the near-revolution of 1968 was just starting. France was ruled by a popular military hero who kept alive the image of *la civilisation française,* though we foreign students knew that the country was run by bureaucrats who had been perfecting their skills of obfuscation, obscurement, and opacity since at least the time of Louis XIV.

It was only twenty years ago that Alyosha gave me my first Chinese name. I remember sitting in his room at the hotel he and Irmtraude lived in in Montparnasse, down the rue Daguerre from where I lived. We would cook on bottled gas burners in their small room. Irmtraude would make her Austrian dishes and Alyosha would recreate the exotic mixtures of his Chinese father and Cambodian mother. As an American, and at that time not much of a cook, I didn't have much skill to contribute, but I did get food from the embassy and the post exchange from time to time, and they were always welcome treats.

Not only was Alyosha one of the first Asian people I got to know well, he was also the only person I'd ever met who had traveled to a land even stranger and more ominous than China. It was there, in Moscow, where he was studying at Patrice Lumumba University, that he had to deal with the immigrant's problem of having a name that didn't fit in. I knew him only by his Chinese name, Huang Sung, the name his father gave him. I always wondered if he had a Khmer name from his mother's people. I either never asked or have forgotten. I suppose that now I'll never know.

Sung told me how, in Russia, he took the name of Alyosha, the saintly, innocent Karamazov brother. I felt the need for a Chinese name so that even if my language study was going slowly, I would have at least one word in the language that I could truly say was mine.

One evening after dinner, I asked him for a Chinese name. I so wanted a name that very moment, but he said that he'd give me one in a day or so. Before too long, but still not as quickly as I wanted, he did indeed find a name for me. Following the custom used in giving names to foreigners, Alyosha took a syllable of my last name and used it as a basis for selecting a Chinese surname. From the "K" in my surname, he gave me the name Ko. In itself, of course, that didn't mean much. It's just a surname like all the others. For a personal name he picked one that sounded Chinese but that no Chinese would ever have had, Ti-wen. It represented a transliteration of my English name, Steven, which was a reasonable way of creating a Chinese name. The word *wen* means literature, elegance, or a pattern, like the hidden pattern in a piece of jade. But the word *ti,* a word no Chinese would dream of using in a name, means emperor or imperial. And so Alyosha, named after the innocent Karamazov brother, named me Imperial Elegance or, perhaps, Imperialist Language.

It didn't much matter and I must have thought it rather funny, especially when we sat at a leftist rally in the great auditorium at the Place Maubert, where leftist rallies always took place, and listened to the traveling choir of the Viet Cong singing songs of revolution. Mr. Imperialist-Language stood with thousands of others and sang the "Internationale" with outstretched arm and clenched fist, as we set the hall trembling with the rhythm of our marching in place and tossed coins into the red flag the Vietnamese held stretched out taut. The idea makes me smile now, twenty-two years later.

Soon after that I went back to the States, and there met what I truly believed would be a new American revolution. Along the way I encountered drugs, Buddhism, university politics, excitement, and boredom. Alyosha Sung and I never stayed in touch much after that. I wonder where he went when he had to leave France. Did he marry Irmtraude and go to Vienna? Somehow I suspect that that city of coffee houses, pastries, and fading memories of the Hapsburgs would not have made such a good home for him. Even the great cultural revolutions that began in Vienna were already either history or orthodoxy by then. So, I wonder, to which of his homes did he go? To China, the land of his father? Did he get to Beijing, and was he there in time for the Red Guards of the Cultural Revolution? Or did he, perhaps, go back to the quiet and peaceful city he so loved, Phnom-Penh? What happened to Alyosha, to his revolution?

I don't know what happened and I never will. I'd like to tell him that as much as I appreciated the name he gave me, I wasn't comfortable with it for too long. Within a couple of years I'd changed it. But for a while, it was me. To have a name meant to have the culture open to me, and for that I must thank Alyosha Huang-sung, or whatever his name might now be, in Cambodia, in China, in Austria, or in France. That is, if he still has a name.

When I left France in 1966, I ended up at the University of Washington in Seattle, where I fell into a circle of students who studied with one of the people who introduced Buddhist thought to the West. Eberhard Julius Dietrich Conze had, on fleeing to England before the outbreak of hostilities, Anglicized his name to Edward. I don't know what happened to the Julius and the Dietrich; they never appeared in any of his English writings.

Dr. Conze taught that form of Buddhism called Perfection of the Wisdom and was responsible for the first comprehensible translations of some of the core texts of the Mahayana. I was one of the lucky ones who were allowed to take his seminars term after term. All of the discourses on the Perfection of Wisdom were full of the most astounding contradictions, illogical statements, and seeming nonsense. Yet these texts spoke to my intellect, and although I was nowhere near ready to recognize it, to my heart. Here I paraphrase one passage: "Truth, truth, as no-truth has this truth been taught by the teacher of truth. . . . Beings, beings, as no-beings have these beings been taught by the teacher. . . . One who is on the spiritual path should produce a thought which is unsupported anywhere, unsupported by forms, unsupported by sounds, unsupported by smells, unsupported by tastes, unsupported by objects of thought."

Such statements excited me and seemed, though incomprehensible, much closer to the way the world really was, or at least ought to be. I'm not sure that I had any sense of what that meant, what the world these texts described was like, but I knew somehow, that it was, if not *the* truth, then at least *a* truth that I wanted to understand.

Dr. Conze had always told us that he was just a *Pandita,* a teacher of words and ideas. What he understood of the teaching, he said, came not from his years of study of Sanskrit and Tibetan texts, but rather from his years spent living in a tiny trailer and growing cabbages as a conscientious objector during the war. If we wanted to understand anything he was teaching us, he said, we would have to find a representative of a living Buddhist tradition with whom to experience Buddhist practice.

My Chinese had progressed to the point where I could make basic conversation. I lacked only the experience of hearing it spoken often and by native speakers. I also needed to do something more about Buddhism than just read about it. In the winter of 1967 I went to California to spend several weeks at the Zen Center's new retreat deep in the mountains of Big Sur. The Center was not open to the public and it was only as Conze's student that I was able to get permission to visit. On the way, I stopped in San Francisco to meet a strange Chinese monk of whom I had heard from a friend in Seattle. My Chinese was shaky, as was I, when I found the address on a narrow street in Chinatown.

Waverly Place was a street that felt as if it existed in some sort of time and space warp. On Grant Avenue in San Francisco you knew clearly that you were in California, USA. Turn the corner to Waverly Place and you were in another decade, if not another continent. The street was home to two Chinese music associations which constantly blared poorly amplified and (I think but never could really tell) poorly played music onto the street. It also had a Taoist-Buddhist popular temple, several laundries and bakeries, three or four Benevolent Associations (which might have been anything from family groups to associations of people who had come from a particular village) and Chinese Mafia fronts. It was hard to tell the difference among these places.

The door to 126 Waverly Place led into a dark and narrow hall. At the end of four flights of stairs was a small landing with a set of doors with frosted glass windows. A scent of incense, though not the sweet Indian or hippie incenses we used so much then, drifted onto the landing. I went into the small temple, the oldest surviving Chinese temple in San Francisco. It was a long narrow room. Panels carved with ornate geometric designs covered the walls, surmounted by a frieze of mythical birds and dragons. At the front of the room was a grand carved altar and screen which extended the full width of the room. Everything that was not covered with badly faded gilt was painted an equally fading vermillion. In the center, the focal point of the shrine, was an old, small image of the popular goddess of southern China, T'ien Hou, the Queen of Heaven. She was draped with robes and festooned with pearls. In front of her, and fully blocking her and the entire shrine from view, was a large and ugly plaster Buddha, crudely and amateurishly made.

At the long table which filled the room sat an old Chinese man with a shaved head. He was wearing what appeared to be yellow pajamas. I later found out that they were part of the standard Chinese monk's uniform. I had sat alone with rabbis before and, although I had always felt a little uncomfortable, I had never felt anything quite like this. I felt as though he looked both at and in some way through me. I wanted to think that it was just my bad Chinese that was making me feel so strange, but I knew that it wasn't. This man knew something that I needed to know.

I stayed overnight and by the morning knew that I would never reach the Zen Center. I told him that I wanted to learn to meditate and that I wanted him to teach me. He pointed to a small stool that faced the wall and told me to sit there and start. He'd be back. He did come back, hours later. His only instructions were, "You like more sitting." By the end of my week's stay there I knew I would become his student and that with him I would learn to meditate. I also asked for a name. The name Alyosha had given me in Paris was no longer appropriate. My focus was already changing from the realm of politics to more contemplative work, and for this I needed a new name.

The day before I left, the monk told me the name he'd selected for me. Like Alyosha, he'd picked a common Chinese surname for me. Like Sung the Abbot (that's what I called Alyosha in those days), he chose a last name that sounded like my western one. This time I was named K'o rather than Ko, and my personal name was one that did, indeed, sound Chinese. It was Erh-k'ang, which means "health, strength, solidity."

I went back to Seattle and studied for another year with Dr. Conze. It was 1968, the year of assassinations, bombings, and riots. Like many of my friends, I expected that the year 1968 would be remembered alongside 1848, except that this time we would win! I looked back at that year of revolution and at other revolutions, and realized that the Buddhists were right when they said that all human action was motivated by greed, anger, and confusion, and that anything that was so motivated was in the end doomed to fail.

The anger which I felt and which ran through all young Americans in those days would, I believed, be enough to bring down the government and change the political and economic order of the country. Throughout the world there were signs of the oncoming revolution. In China the Red Guards were marching. In Czechoslovakia the Prague Spring burst forth. Back in Paris, my friends seemed about to bring down the Fifth Republic. The sick age of imperialist government was about to end and the new age of healthy and strong spiritual community was about to start. It was obvious. Everyone could see it, couldn't they?

I knew about what had happened in France in the period of the Terror after the Revolution. In the great revolution of our century, Russia had gone from the terror of the czar to another terror. Revolution based only on political ends was always followed by intolerance and purges. This time, I felt, there was a need for a revolution that recognized the spiritual basis of all the changes of the sixties. By 1970, I was sure, the revolution would have taken hold, and in five years it would have recognized its need for a spiritual base. Then, the initial wave of politics over, the call would go out for people to articulate the spiritual foundation of revolution. Those of us who had chosen the monasteries and ashrams over the barricades and bombs would emerge and help the revolution realize its political ends in a spiritual way.

To get ready for that time, I became a monk, and received two more names. The first of these was the name the Abbot gave me when I formally became a disciple of his. The system of Chinese names places their owners clearly in a lineage. Each family has a long poem inscribed in the family annals. Each new generation takes the next word in the poem as the first syllable of its name. Thus, all the siblings and cousins in one generation will share one syllable of their name. Each will also have one syllable which is his or hers alone. The effect of this system is to ensure that all names have meaning, and that there is a lineage of meaning between the genera-

1. MY FAVORITE ROOM/*Lindsay Cobb*
("Childhood," chapter 5)

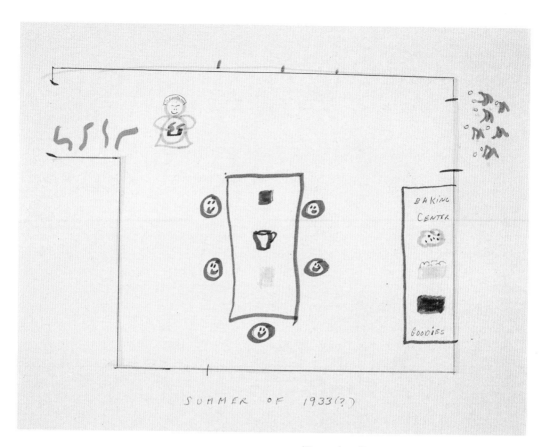

SUMMER OF 1933(?)

## 2. KITCHEN SCENE/*Lorraine Lee*
### ("Childhood," chapter 5)

Explanation: The scene takes place in my maternal grandmother's kitchen. Five grandchildren (all siblings) have just come in from the beach abutting our grandparents' home. (Note the sand and water washed off feet outside of back entry in upper righthand portion of sketch.)

The children sit at the table, which contains butter, homemade currant and raspberry jelly, and a pitcher of milk. Grandma carries a fresh-baked loaf of bread from the oven. As I explained this picture at the workshop, it suddenly struck me as a communion-like ritual where "Priestess" Grandma serves bread and milk to her beloved grandchildren.

The baking center on the right denotes Grandma's early-morning production of breadstuffs: pies, cakes, coffeecakes, etc., ordered by the neighbors. Grandpa was out of work for a while during the Depression (the scene takes place in 1933) and Grandma assured some cash flow by her considerable "German housewife" baking skills.

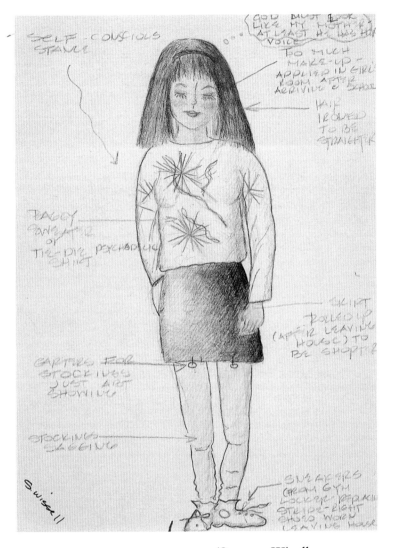

**3. SELF-PORTRAIT**/*Susanne Wissell*

("Adolescence," chapter 6)

Artist's comments (beginning at upper left, reading clockwise):
"Self-conscious stance; 'God must look like my mother—at least He
has her voice . . .'; Too much makeup—applied in girls' room after
arriving at school; Hair ironed to be straighter; Skirt rolled up (after
leaving house) to be shorter; Sneakers (from gym locker) replacing
Stride-Rite shoes worn leaving house; Stockings sagging; Garters
for stockings just about showing; Baggy sweater or tie-dye psyche-
delic shirt."

4. SELF-PORTRAIT/*Marilee Crocker*
("Adolescence," chapter 6)

5. IMAGE OF GOD/*Dan Wakefield*
("Adolescence," chapter 6)

6. "CORKY"/*Dan Wakefield*
("Friend/Mentor/Teacher," chapter 7)

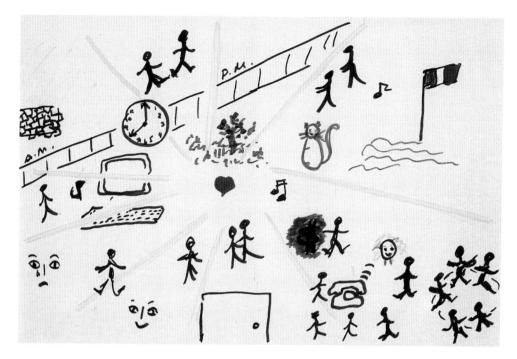

7. THE PRESENT/*Jane Redmont*
("How to Do It," chapter 4)

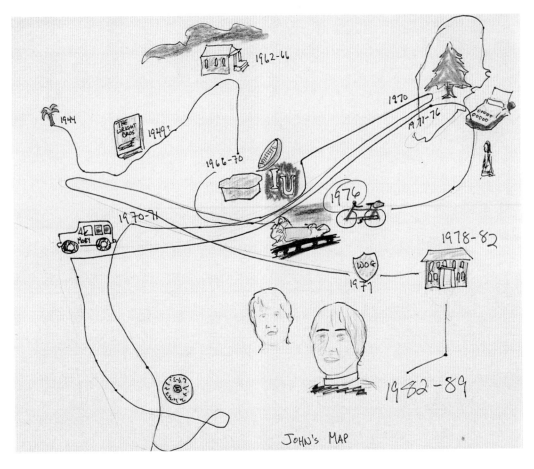

8. ROAD MAP/*John Gould*

("A Road Map of Your Spiritual Journey," chapter 8)

tions. When you meet someone else with a similar name you can automatically tell if you are related.

In this system my name was Kuo Ning. The character *kuo* means fruition, result, or effect. *Ning* means peace, tranquility, or stillness. Together with the K'ang of the first name the Abbot had given me, the compound K'ang Ning means physically strong, robust, and quiet. Later, when I was fully ordained, I was given another name, Heng Ching. The character *heng* is a generation name meaning constant, long-term. *Ching* has much the same meaning as *ning,* and together the two words form a compound which means tranquil, quiet, still, at peace.

I would spend thirteen years with those Chinese names. During that time the revolution would not happen, yet its values would in some way affect the fabric of American life. The war would end and some of us would take credit, probably more than we deserved, for ending it. The government wouldn't fall but two presidents would. The old order wouldn't vanish but it would change.

Steven was gone. Etienne had only appeared at times in France when I was being silly. Ko' Ti-wen, Alyosha's pseudo Chinese name for me, disappeared with him, first into Paris and then into who knows where. But one name, Shmuel ben-David, was in the background and would reappear.

———

**POLLY BATES**   Polly Bates was working as an associate editor of publications at Simmons College when the course was going on. She and her husband came to hear a reading I gave at Harvard that December, and we had coffee afterward in Harvard Square and enjoyed a talk about what we all were reading at the time. When I spoke with Polly recently, she was expecting her first child, and preparing to move to Washington, where her husband Stephen had been appointed to a legal clerkship. She has a genuine sense of "centeredness" that comes across with quiet strength in her story.

*Coming to Shore*   When I was a young girl and had only recently begun attending church, I remember asking my dad if Father Don, our minister, was God. It made sense to me. After all, during the service he stood at the front of the church in his somber robes with a lavish Christ figure behind him and candles dripping on either side, while we in the congregation faced him, responding in unison to his prayers. I thought when we spoke of God as "He" or "Our Father" we were talking about Father Don. Though my dad tried to explain the misunderstanding to me, saying that Father Don was only a conduit to God, I remained puzzled. The underlying concept was too abstract for me to understand.

My confusion faded over time as the prayers and hymns, through countless repetitions, became second nature to me. I didn't think about what the words meant—whatever solace they offered was simply due to their familiarity. But unconsciously, I internalized the words so that they came to define my religious beliefs. As a member of the choir, I particularly enjoyed the grandeur of the holiday processionals—the incense, the organ, the church packed with familiar faces, all confirmed my sense of belonging.

It wasn't until I was a senior in college and took a course called "A Feminist Perspective on Religion" that I questioned the severe limitations of the language of the Episcopal church, and saw how they had affected my outlook on religion. The class was unlike anything else I had taken. We met in the evening in a lounge, a dozen of us sprawled on old sofas and the floor. The teacher, an ex-nun who had left the church to marry and raise a family, was thoughtful and objective. She made me see religion in a whole new light. For the first time I understood that the term "Our Father" was simply a metaphor for God; the words were meant not to define God as a kindly patriarch looking down on us, but rather to lend some accessibility and humanity to the purely abstract. When this idea struck me, I realized how all those years the male-gendered language had unconsciously formed my sense of God. Replacing those words with "She" and "Our Mother" gave me an entirely different sense of the deity. All the prayers I was brought up on, the hymns and Bible readings, had conjured up a false version of God, a male version that overlooked me.

After this epiphany of sorts, I found I was no longer comfortable in church. It had been quite a while since I'd gone anyway—I had stopped once I left for college. But now when I attended church at Christmas time with my family, I felt not just uninspired, but angry and removed. The words did not speak to me, they excluded me. Sitting in church, all I saw were the men swaggering around in front—the minister, the acolytes, the lay readers—and all I heard about was the male God we were supposed to be praying to. The cloying incense, the chants, the extravagant robes now seemed oddly barbaric to me. There wasn't a place for me there. I no longer thought of the Episcopal church as mine, a realization that both liberated and unnerved me.

This progression from believer to agnostic may sound more straightforward than it was. In actuality, the church had never played much of a role in my spiritual life. Growing up, the lengthy service was more something to endure than to actively experience. I whiled away the hour with concerns about my appearance, thoughts about other people's appearance, and daydreams of what I'd do when I got home. I always envied the people who, eyes shut in prayer, seemed transported to another plane. I wanted to know what secret words they whispered that seemed to take them closer to God. Even after college, I never stopped wanting to have a faith; I just stopped looking for one, especially in church.

For the most part, the few moments of spiritual inspiration I've experienced have been tied to nature. Neither prompted nor performed by rote like the prayers said in church, these moments have always taken me by surprise, filling me with an exquisite, wordless joy.

I remember one such evening up at my family's cottage in Ontario. Having just finished my senior year of high school, I was vacationing with my parents for several weeks before resuming my soda-jerk job at Baskin-Robbins. The cottage, a modest boxy construction, hunkered high on a hill overlooking Indian Lake. The hillside was covered with fir trees, the ground beneath them blanketed with dry and fragrant needles, soft and worn as sand. The second evening after dinner, I slipped down to the lake and perched at the end of the dock, gazing out over the shimmering water. Several lights twinkled at the opposite shore a mile away; above me, I could make out the Big and Little Dippers. Occasionally in the distance a boat would skirt past—I could just decipher its red and green taillight and the fading whinny of its motor. Now and then, breaking the peaceful silence, a loon would cry, the tremulous notes reverberating around the lake, achingly fragile and beautiful. It was my graduation night. In an auditorium back home the five hundred members of my senior class, in blue and gold caps and gowns, were lining up to get their diplomas. I had chosen instead to come here with my parents, and I didn't regret it. In fact, sitting by the water, embraced by the clear overarching sky, I felt closer to those students than I ever had. Any grievances I had with the past four fairly awful years of school evaporated. I felt I had everything before me, and I was optimistic and ready.

Spiritual times such as this, when I am totally caught in the present moment and have shrugged off any self-consciousness, are rare for me. Far more often I find myself caught up in the mundane details and concerns of daily living. I have gone through vast chunks of my life as though submerged under water, without giving a passing thought to a God or faith or anything larger than myself and those I love. Occasionally I've popped up above water, gasping for breath and realizing frantically that I need to find something more. But, looking around briefly for inspiration and finding none, tired of treading water, I slowly sink under once more and return to oblivion. This oblivion isn't despairing. Though I have had some bad moments, my life for the most part has been quite fortunate. Still, underlying this contentment has been an increasingly nagging desire for a spiritual underpinning that would make my life more permanent, somehow, and more meaningful. Events over the past few months have brought home to me the pressing need to find this spiritual center without delay.

Last June I went with my mother to visit my grandmother in Vancouver. I hadn't seen her in sixteen years. It's hard to say what happened to all those years: time just seemed to slip away. I was excited yet anxious at the prospect of revisiting my parents' hometown and seeing my grandmother. My feelings toward her were bound up in memory. All these years, she had stayed alive for me only in adolescent recollections— I clearly remembered her beautiful house in the country with the goldfish pond and the little guest house containing the antique organ. The few visits my brother and I had there were happy. But she and my grandfather had long ago sold the house to move to an apartment; he had since died and she now lived in a nursing home. Returning to Vancouver was almost like going back in time to a place that no longer existed. I had no idea what to expect.

When my mother and I got to the nursing home, we discovered that Nana was in the hospital, so we drove there. After some delay at the front desk, we found her in the emergency ward—the hospital was overcrowded so they had had to tuck her away in one of the curtained cubicles. My mom went in first—I waited awkwardly in the hall, trying not to look at the other patients lying vulnerable in their beds, exposed to all passersby. Beckoned in, I nervously approached the bed. My grandmother's face looked the same; though her hair was sparser, her eyes were still clear and bright blue. But her shrunken body was like a child's—it barely ruffled the sheets. She'd always been a slim, regal woman who stood straight with her shoulders back. Now she was slightly slumped over, with several different tubes attached to her thin wrists. I hugged her gently as she said my name. She was ninety-five and I was thrilled that she knew who I was. Without realizing it, both my mother and I had started to cry. It seemed so miraculous that I would see Nana again after all this time, and yet so appallingly sad that all those years had swept by. So much had happened to me—from the time I was thirteen until now at twenty-nine—that she knew nothing about. Clearly, she wasn't going to live much longer; certainly I wouldn't visit her again. The last time I saw her that week she had been moved to a hospital room with three other women, one of whom loudly watched television all day. With her husband and friends dead and her only child living three thousand miles away, Nana would be truly alone when we left. She had no one to visit her; the days would just drift by in a befuddled haze of sleep and pain. It was very hard to say goodbye. I was already grieving, not just for losing Nana then, but for all the years together we had already lost.

It seemed such a meaningless waste. Flying home, I wondered what the point of having family was if you never knew them, never lived your lives with them. It became clear to me that nothing of importance ought to be postponed; that the time to act, if I cared, was now.

As my thirtieth birthday approached, this feeling intensified. As I've said, most of the time my concern about spiritual life has been relegated to the back of my mind, somewhere behind other good intentions like reading the classics and learning self-defense. I always assumed that eventually I would develop a solid faith and that, much like my mother, I would have children and raise them unquestioningly in a church I felt securely a part of. But with my thirtieth birthday on the horizon, I realized that these things weren't just going to fall into place on their own. Time was passing—my biological and spiritual clocks were ticking. Going to Vancouver had made me see that I couldn't waste any more time. I had to make a concerted effort now to sort out my feelings about God.

Deciding to take this course—actually picking up the phone and registering—was one of the hardest things I've done in recent years. As much as I urgently felt the need to confront my spiritual life, I was afraid that I might find nothing there, and that having tried and failed, I would give up forever on the hope for a deeper existence. But that hasn't happened. The class assignments and discussion have forced me to consider my spiritual past and I have found things there that I had long thought forgotten. It has also helped crystallize my desire for a more spiritual future. Equally important, the class has given me the opportunity to talk with others who care about such matters, and that is a tremendous release. My closest friends, though generally open to new ideas, are curiously uninterested in the spiritual dimension of life, so that I feel constrained in talking to them about it. And others, if the subject comes up, seem noticeably uncomfortable.

My parents recently visited at Thanksgiving. One day, the three of us seated comfortably in a restaurant for lunch, I thought I'd take the opportunity to figure out something that had puzzled me. When I was younger, my father, who had diligently sung in the church choir for as long as I could remember, abruptly and permanently left the church. He is a thoughtful man of integrity. I thought if I knew why he had left, it could help me understand my own ambivalence. So in the middle of lunch, out of the blue, I asked, "Dad, do you remember when it was you stopped going to church?" Pausing a moment and looking surprised, he told me it had been twelve years. His face was guarded and the atmosphere had become constrained. I knew that he didn't want to talk about it, so I quickly changed the subject. It was then that I fully realized that I would have to untangle my spiritual past, and chart my future, by myself.

Over the past few months, I feel as though I've gradually pulled my head above water. Forays to various local churches have helped me sort out what I'm looking for. I realize that in striving for a spiritual life, I'm seeking not just a deep connection to God, but a connection to other people as well. Certainly I'm nowhere near having the well-integrated spiritual life I hope for. But at least I have a destination now, a shore towards which I'm swimming strongly.

———————

MARY     Mary describes herself as "a forty-two-year-old public relations specialist, jewelry maker, and hospice volunteer who tries to remember what is really important in life." If natural cheer and good humor are important in life, Mary has succeeded in remembering. She is one of those people whose presence puts others at ease, and whose brightness and energy are contagious. She is a co-owner of the great old Victorian house she lives in, where she entertained our ongoing group with a great summer meal of homemade health food delicacies. Her concern for others is reflected in her own spiritual autobiography.

*A Gift from Mother Teresa*

It was 26 December 1987, my birthday. We were driving up to the house in Calcutta where Mother Teresa lived. I felt as if I was walking into one of my most wonderful dreams. Even though our tour guide said she was rarely in, I knew she would be there today. I always knew I would meet her someday.

As we entered the convent where she lived, we walked past the beggars waiting in line for food and the children with runny noses and outstretched hands asking us for "bon bons."

The walls of the convent were bare and clean. There was only one very simply printed sign that read, "Unless you are as a little child, you will not enter the Kingdom of God."

The nuns wore the blue and white habits of Mother Teresa's Sisters of Charity. They walked with purpose and smiled politely. They were not surprised to see a group of twenty Americans in their home.

The house was immaculate, a contrast to the filth of the streets. This was one of the few places I felt there was breathing space, so different from the overcrowding of the streets of Calcutta. The house was filled with the blue and white of the Sisters and not the vivid colors of the streets—the orange and red spices displayed for sale, the gaudily painted buses, the married women with red dye on the parts in their hair so that they would be sure to keep their passion within and only for their husbands.

Our guide went to see if Mother Teresa was in. He came back a few minutes later with a smile on his face and excitement in his voice. "She is in, and if we are lucky she will wave to us. She is too busy these days to meet with many people." He pointed across a courtyard to her room.

We watched as the Sisters prepared huge vats of food. They made it look simple, although this meal, it seemed, would feed hundreds. I remembered the wild woman I became when I had to cook for six.

Then we saw Mother Teresa come from her room. She had a meeting with two women from Poland, our guide told us.

She sat with them and signed some papers. It seemed enough just to see her from where we stood. She finished her business, and then walked over and started talking as if she had expected us all along. I was in front of the line. She asked me my name and where I came from. She said she was happy we had time to visit with her.

"We do the work of God here," she began. "We believe that no one should come into this world without love, nor should anyone die without love, and that is what we can offer here. This is what we all can offer." She smiled. "Here we love until it hurts. Please pray for us and pray for a cure for AIDS. You know that our Sisters are founding missions in your country to care for persons with AIDS."

She thanked us once again for coming and shook each of our hands. I felt like crying, but I thought I was the only one who would feel that, since it was me who had talked about coming to her house from the moment we got on the plane to India. I had been so convincing that our Calcutta tour was changed so that we could all come here.

I turned and looked at the members of our group when I got to the door. Everyone was in tears.

Another Sister invited us to take a tour of their orphanage. We saw children who looked healthier than many of the children of the streets of India. They called us "Auntie," and rushed to us with outstretched arms. They bathed us in hugs.

Photography was not allowed, but if it had been I would have snapped a group of twenty two-year olds sitting in a circle and waving to us. I wondered why they were sitting so quietly and then realized they were all on potty chairs, perfectly still except for occasional tiny giggles. They were so happy to see us that they waved for five minutes, except for one little girl. She looked at us with panic, and it was explained to us that she was frightened by our white skin.

As I look back I wonder why India, and more specifically meeting Mother Teresa, was a highlight of my spiritual journey. In India I saw poverty and squalor and tragedy—mothers who maimed their children so they would get more money from begging—but I also saw people living in community and helping one another. There was a code of ethics even among beggars. The disabled were allowed the first "go-round" at begging. If they didn't have enough to eat, it was explained to us, the other beggars would take care of them.

As we drove through the countryside, I realized that prosperity didn't mean owning a $45,000 car or a house with a white picket fence in the country, but rather a good crop, food to feed one's family. I saw the pride the women took in their saris, the colored cloths that painted the landscapes in canary yellows and electric blues. I knew they didn't have closets full of clothes; they had only one sari and often no shoes. Many took pride in their children and in their homes, too. I realized this as I watched a man furiously sweeping the dirt from his one-room open shack. He piled all the dirt and papers in a wastebasket and then walked immediately outside his house and dumped the garbage. Although the streets were unbearably dirty, the people weren't.

India helped me crystallize a value system that has been evolving throughout the years: the value of community, of appreciating. The words of Gandhi echoed in my mind: "If I don't see God in the next person I meet, I am not living correctly."

Mother Teresa said, "Loneliness is worse than poverty." I had grown up an only child: a lonely life. My father was an alcoholic, and my mother abandoned me to him. My memories of childhood were going to bars with him, scared of the men in the bars, bailing him out of jail. My mother told me, every day it seemed, that I wasn't good enough, that no one would like me because of the way I looked. I never could do anything right for her although I tried so hard. I would have been willing to do anything to make her happy, but I never seemed to know what it was.

I can now look back on that part of my journey and realize that I would never be the person I am today if I hadn't had that path. If nothing else, it has made it easier for me to empathize with a lot of people. I have come to respect the importance and validity of each person's unfolding journey. I don't try to save them from the pain of it as I once used to do.

How did I survive? How did any of us survive? I look back at where grace was in my life. There was always someone or something that was there as a saving grace. My Aunt Flora, my Uncle Dave, my books, my writing.

What motivated my life when I was younger was to accumulate experiences, so I went off to Europe at age twenty-two. It opened my eyes to the world more than anything else I had done up to that point. Spirituality was in art and music. At that point in my life, friends were dispensable. I needed no one.

My world changed when I was twenty-eight. My mother died suddenly of a heart attack and my father, who was sick for as long as I can remember, had congestive heart failure. I took care of him for two years. Then he died. I remember thinking the pain would never go away. I admired people who lived into their seventies with all the pain that life must bring.

One year later I moved to another city. I then realized that I was really all alone, an only child with no family to run home to. I hadn't really cultivated many friendships. I felt very alone and frightened, frightened I wouldn't make it. I wasn't sure what not making it meant, maybe sitting in my chair and never moving again.

But again grace was in my life. There were people there, almost miraculously, when I hit bottom. I had one friend who was there for me whenever I needed her. I prayed for the courage to pull myself through. Although my personal life was falling apart, I was able to perform my work. I went into counseling and learned a lot about myself. That was when my faith really began to grow. It was always there even though I wouldn't have admitted it.

I did public relations for a hospital and wrote articles for a community magazine. I chose articles that would help me work out my own "stuff." I remember that Hemingway used his typewriter as a therapist. I did stories on child abuse, childhood depression, incest. I worked so passionately at them and then realized I was trying to save the world from the awfulness that I had experienced.

After only fourteen months at that job, something happened that crushed my confidence almost completely. I had to find another job, but I was sure I wouldn't survive without the help of my built-in friends at work. I thought they would never remain my friends. I was devastated, but again grace was at work, although I didn't see it. I guess I never see it except in hindsight. Within two months I had a job with a better title and $1,000 more a month in salary, and I loved it. What seemed like an awful event turned into opportunity.

One day a friend of mine was making a week-long directed retreat—which meant complete silence—and asked if I would like to go. I had four weeks' vacation and I thought maybe it wouldn't be so bad. After all, it was near the ocean . . . and cheap! But I was frightened, frightened of being quiet for a week, of facing myself. I guess my image was of shriveling up and dying.

I went prepared to go into sensory deprivation. I brought at least twenty books, writing paper, a quilt to crochet and oils to paint even though I had never picked up a paintbrush in my life.

During the week I never picked up any of my "toys." I was silent for the week, meeting only once daily with a priest who helped me look at where I was in my life. This was the first time in my life into which I hadn't scheduled frantic activity. Although I was alone, I felt more filled than I ever had. I looked at nature, I listened, and I heard.

By this time I was choosing to write articles on friendship, touch, humor, and nurturing the child within. No longer was I working out my past. Instead, I was looking for ways to live more fully.

After my retreat, in fact, two weeks after, I knew that I wanted to become a counselor, so I did research, took the necessary tests, and enrolled in a program, all within a month.

It took three years of agony for me because I had to take risks. It was an experiential program, and I was constantly having to put myself out in front of people. I grew more than I could ever have imagined. I took risks and gave workshops on the power of humor, the benefits of touch, the art of living. It was incredible for me to be doing this, because I was always someone who hid behind my writing, and here I was talking about humor on television and radio!

Just before I gave my first workshop I went on another retreat. How would I ever get up in front of a group of people and teach? I was the student who was always hollered at in school because I wouldn't answer. I just didn't have enough confidence, but I thought it was because I was stupid.

While meditating on my upcoming workshop one evening during the retreat, an image came to me. It was the feeling of being held in the palms of someone's hands. It was a powerful image and it stayed with me. It was certainly reassuring.

Before my first evening talk, my best friend, another life-saving friend who really believed in me, asked if she could do meditation with me. She knew my panic. She closed her eyes and said a prayer, and then asked if it was all right if she could do something that had just come to her. She massaged the muscles in my neck which, by this time, had almost atrophied from stress. She did this and then she held my head in her hands. It was the same feeling, the same image I had had during my retreat.

I knew I would be OK. I was, and without ever asking to do another workshop, I was invited to give many more of them for three years until it was time for me to take another path. My prayer during graduate school was Saint Francis's "Make me an instrument of your peace" prayer. I felt it was coming true.

I learned to trust a bit more. If there was something I needed to say either in the articles I was writing or in my workshops, the information always found me. It is an incredible experience to watch how this unfolds, and yet when I am in it, I am usually skeptical. "It worked for me last time, but this time I just won't get the article done," my thought process goes.

I did hospice work and followed a fifty-three-year-old woman with a brain tumor. I loved the work; I felt instrumental in helping her and her family. I realized I was replaying the helper role that I had played in my family. And my spirituality deepened even more as someone allowed me to share their dying experience.

After I had done four articles with different titles on the value of friendship, I realized that friends and people are a very important part of my life. I invested in them, and they have become as precious to me as my signed picture of Mother Teresa. One of the most wonderful things I have learned from my friends is that I can be me, me with all my faults, and they will still accept me. I can fight and be irrational and they still accept me.

I am learning that I am always taken care of even though sometimes I get very frightened. When it seems like life is overwhelming, I just turn it over to God and say OK, do with me as you wish. It works—when I remember!

Recently I looked back on my forty-two years and wondered what I would regard as my accomplishments. Almost without fail, it has to do with people, with being there for them, with helping them grow. This surprised me; I would have thought it would have been college degrees or awards or other compliments the world can give you.

I believe strongly in the healing power of forgiveness and I am constantly working on it in my own life. I still battle with the fear of being alone, but it has taught me how to pray often.

In India, I learned the meaning of *namaste,* the word used for greetings and for saying goodbye. It means: I recognize the God in you, and if you are at that place, and I am at that place, then there is only one of us.

*Namaste.*

———

**ANONYMOUS** A modest member of our class who is a person of great integrity as well as reserve asked to be identified only as "a woman in her mid-thirties" who wishes to remain anonymous. With respect and regard, I honor the wish, with appreciation for her moving and honest account.

## *Losses and Gains*

One Monday in March 1987, I suddenly lost my job. I had gone to work at seven thirty that morning and at noon I was told to leave. My boss told me the company was reorganizing and wouldn't need me anymore. I had no choice. I just had to leave. I did, hurrying out, too shocked and upset to even say goodbye to my staff.

The memory of this loss is so clear to me that I feel as though it just happened. I had worked as a supervisor for almost two years at this company and during that time I had felt as if I had finally started to make something of myself. I felt a bit special because the company was new and I was part of the team which would hire and train most of the other employees. I had finally taken a risk, getting a job which required me to be more outgoing. I had been determined to get a job less isolating than my previous ones. At times, though, I felt overwhelmed by how outgoing and assertive I had to be. I had never managed people before and some of them intimidated me. But at least I was learning something new. I kept all my fears and doubts to myself.

The job grew frustrating. The company was in a financial crisis and I found myself without the help I needed. Everyone was overworked. I was spending so much time at the job that I grew close to the other supervisors. We went out to lunch every day and spent much of our free time together. For the first time in my life, I rarely felt lonely. My friendships with these four women made up for all my frustrations on the job.

On the Monday my job ended, I was in shock. I remember asking my boss if one of my friends could drive me home. I was afraid I might cry if I had to take the bus home alone. My friends Judy and Linda drove me, telling me as they dropped me off to get a lot of wine. They would be over after work. I went upstairs to my apartment, opened a beer, and called a professor I had had in college. I had just talked with her a couple of days before. I can't remember what either of us said, but I know I needed to talk to someone. Then I called my mother. I can't remember what she said either, but once I hung up, I felt calm. I happily went to the store for wine.

My friends came over that night. We sat around my table and complained about my unfair fate. They talked of quitting their own jobs. I felt a strange sense, though, that our camaraderie was already beginning to change. In one of our quiet moments I heard the truth in the back of my mind: I had no job. I was no longer part of the group.

I had never imagined losing a job. Although I knew it was a common experience, I thought out of fear that I would be exempt, that God would make sure such a trauma would never happen to me. But it did happen. At first I didn't acknowledge how abandoned I felt. I was numb. I prayed to God to help me find another job. I was so scared that I went to the Catholic church on Arch Street and lit candles. I prayed to whatever saint I saw statues of. All this seemed to work, because three weeks later I got another job. Everyone I knew, including myself, was amazed at how fast I found it. I felt relieved and grateful.

I started my new job a month after I had lost the old one. The first day went well, I thought, because I didn't cry when I got home as I usually did with new jobs. After the week ended, though, I started to feel depressed. The protective shock was wearing off. I missed my old friends and the familiarity of my old job. I was uncomfortable working for a bank. The rules and language were so different from the ones at the insurance companies where I had always worked. After about a month, I felt more lost than I ever had in my life. My confidence started to disappear. Tension grew between my old friends and me. I had secretly expected them to show their loyalty by quitting their jobs. Of course they didn't. We started to lose touch as I withdrew into myself. No one at my new job was friendly. My life was a mess.

During this time I began feeling desperate for some place to belong. I had never felt so rejected before. I was still going to the Catholic church every Sunday and I started going with even more need for God's protection. After a while, though, I began to feel unwelcome. I felt that God was angry at me, and that he had let me lose my job to punish me. He took away my friends. He left me. For the first time I doubted the God I had grown up with. I had never felt so alone.

I began to think that maybe I should look for God somewhere else, in another church. I needed faith in something, especially since I had lost it in myself and in my friends. This scared me, though, because I had never left the Catholic church. I often hated the politics of the Church. Its concern for power and control has scared me. I thought that if I left the church I would be punished, just as the nuns of my childhood had warned. I already felt punished, so I stayed in the Church, afraid of what other trauma might happen. This year, though, I have started to leave. The threat of God's wrath still lingers, but I am slowly giving up my childhood fears. I am reluctant to admit that, at thirty-four, I am just starting to leave my childhood church.

I don't think I have ever felt so confused before. The Catholic church had always given me a sense of certainty. I needed this sense of stability when I was a child, because my father suffered from schizophrenia and he was unpredictable. I was never sure what was going to happen to my family. At any moment I thought my father would leave and never come back. Or I thought he might stay and act strangely. I spent much time in my childhood trying to anticipate the day before it began. Catholic school helped me in this because we did the same things every day. The routine nurtured me in a way my family didn't. It gave me a sense of control which I carried through my life. Going to church every Sunday and being diligent at my work during the week convinced me that I would never fall apart. When I lost my job, everything lost the certainty I had always counted on.

These days my confusion has brought me both despair and joy in a way I have never experienced before. Without my old definition of God, I am going to different churches on Sunday. Sometimes I feel uncomfortable about my break with the past. Without the familiar rituals and language, I feel out of touch with the God who once meant so much. I panic sometimes, thinking I will never experience a deep connection again. I get scared as I realize how much my life has changed, and that I no longer know who I am, who God is. Yet amid all this turmoil, I sometimes see God more than ever, outside the Church. The sight of late afternoon light in autumn brings me a sense of joy I cannot describe. I feel this way when I see wildflowers along a wall, red berries in a hedge, or a sky clearing after a storm. I suddenly feel deeply about the small pieces of life. They are all the more valuable because I have had to lose so much to find them.

———————

**ELENA ADELAIDE**

Elena Adelaide is the pen name of a woman who writes that she "has spent the past eight years in banking, as a 'maverick' without any of the implied romance. Her previous life was dedicated to writing. Over the past decade and through Dan's class, she has struggled to return writing and her spirit to the center of her life." Elena Adelaide is one of the people whose wit, which shows in her eyes, graciously saved us from taking ourselves too seriously. Her special love and appreciation of poetry shines through her paper.

*The Wider Life*

I stopped writing more than ten years ago. Since that time, I've taken one class, at the University of Massachusetts at Boston, in which I simply reworked earlier pieces. By that time, I had finally succeeded in snuffing out my identity. As both a part of that process and a consequence of it, I could no longer stir the ashes of my spirit into a spark to be put down on paper.

When I was eleven years old, I surprised my math teacher by doing a project on the Möbius strip, a topological phenomenon. I've come to think of it as a rectangular strip of space with only one surface: no top, bottom, or sides. If its ends are connected, a Möbius strip becomes an eternal circle which holds a single set of points, twisting and bending in time. Its beginning and end points are lost when they become part of the single-surfaced whole.

Similarly, my "life map" reflects the points of a single spiritual struggle: to achieve rebirth through death. The synchronicity of many events in my life—which took place all over the world—spoke to and goaded that struggle.

Over the past seven years, my striving to become what I am, find what I see, play music to what I hear has culminated in decisions to put to sleep core parts of my self, grief for my old self, fear of birth and the unknown, and apprehension at the prospect of self-parenting.

During this class, I've read my journal writings and letters from the past twenty years, and pinned to the walls photographs of myself that were taken over the course of thirty-three years. This has been a part of my effort to chronicle my spiritual journey or, more accurately, to recognize it. I'd like to share pieces of it with you, including the poetry of others, since my love for poetry is the most godlike gift I've known. My father gave it to me.

My father was not able to invoke the promise of springtime or give me the gifts of perspective and self-love. Instead, he gave me curiosity and a deep, passionate love of poetry, which, since childhood, has run through my veins and kept my heart filled.

In 1974, the first assignment of my first college writing class was to simulate the interior monologue of a child.

under my covers it's my fig fat quilt and Mommy pulls it up over my head      I scream and make her be careful she doesn't touch me      her hands are so cold      she says her fingers are piano fingers and she used to play but stopped because after a while you don't have time to do everything and she covers my head      I don't breathe or move the whole time I make believe I'm already asleep.

Daddy comes in whenever I'm sick I call for Daddy cause his hands are soft and he talks to me and takes out my splinters      the lights are out and Daddy tells me about Raggedy Ann and Humperdink whose two brothers wiped the marshmallow all over his mouth while he was asleep and his mother thought he ate it and she spanked him and his brothers laughed

there sometimes is a nickel under my pillow that Daddy says Johnny Gruell the man who made up Raggedy Ann stories left for me      Johnny Gruell lived in England Daddy was in England during the war      it's dark and it drizzles but Daddy loved it so much and wanted to stay even after the war but things are so you can't do what you want and its too late Daddy says      do you think Johnny Gruell knows about me?

I think Johnny Gruell is dead      my dolls are uncom-

fortable cause they have to sleep sitting up and my room is
big    when it's dark these big circles are rolling at me all
colors and they get bigger than my room and my house
and I'm afraid I'm gonna die if I fall asleep

In 1980, I wrote:

On my twenty-fifth birthday, I sit looking out at the city
trees and a fat Italian lady pulling her wash in off the line
. . . just opened birthday cards, copied the poem "Cynara"
for Diane and written David another "I QUIT!" letter.

I don't want to hurt anymore. Oh, this is the year for
throwing off the last of the family shackles, for taking flight.
I'm scared, it's slow, it's painful, it's not going to get me a
pat on the back or a wink of approval from a handsome
man. But it will give me hold of the last remnants of my
life that I have not yet reclaimed as mine—mine for me;
me for me.

So, happy birthday to me, to the fighter and the survivor
and the child that loves M & M's and maraschino cherries
and pretty handsome men with a glint in the eye and sharp
tongues. Happy birthday to the woman who will learn to
love what is good for her and what makes her grow and
shine and see how good she is.

Oh, this is the year to feel my pulse again, to fight for
myself against myself . . . to win and to shout it out loud.

In 1983, I fasted and lost a lot of weight. I wrote in a letter
to a friend:

I'm reading a wonderful book by a woman who went to
Duke for the rice diet and lost her weight as rapidly as I
am losing mine. I find myself crying at times when I realize
the tremendous impact of my fat on my life—its importance—and the equally tremendous effects of giving it up.
Letting the fat person die—who was as much a friend as
an enemy. It's a kind of mourning for me, since my every
minute for the past few years has been 98 percent filled

with her thoughts and feelings of sorrow, self-hatred and pain. The writer of this book [*Winning the Losing Battle* by Eda LeShane] put it so beautifully:

"Half way through [my fast] my exultant mood seemed to slip away quite suddenly. I began to feel very sad. . . . Then something very strange happened: I found myself weeping—in a state of mourning for 'Fat Eda!' That person was *me* for at least forty-five years. . . . She brought me here—but she's going to die here. She willed her own death.

"Suddenly, I was overwhelmed with love and grief. The fat person I was suffered so much and tried so hard. She went on and on, inexorably in search of answers . . . never giving up—and then making the final sacrifice, to die here, so that someone new could live. 'Thin Eda'—who will she be? Will I like her? It is terrifying. The old self is safe, familiar, although full of pain; the new is strange, wonderful, but frightening.

"I feel a wave of love for that self I am leaving forever. She tried her best to take care of me—she brought me to this place—she saved my life. She was not a bad person. She was not lazy or weak. She suffered so much pain.

"If I am suddenly too delighted with myself, I will be avoiding something of equal importance. There is a kind of death going on here, and I must pay attention to it."

It's hard. Sometimes. And no "facts" of what the future will hold. We all recognize the elements of life beyond our physical selves—those are the questions. Will I still be set on guilt and pain? Will I let myself be free? WILL I BE ABLE TO CARRY A TUNE? WILL LESLIE HOWARD COME BACK FROM THE DEAD TO MARRY ME?

Last year, I began to address the very painful and mysterious issue of having experienced sexual assault. I wrote to a friend:

So, this is at the bottom of it all: I am the unspeakable; I am what they write about in college texts; what talk show hosts get misty over; the sin of sins. How could this be me? How could I have missed it? How can I believe it? What do I do with it? How do I live with this? How do I live a life without warmth and comfort or touch? Cold. Remote. The mystique I carry with me is hardly worth it.

Later I wrote:

I'm numb. Nothing reaches into me. Nothing matters. A pebble tossed in a pond does not cause ripples. It does not disturb the universe. All I know is that my furniture is rearranged and my plants are watered.

I am empty. I've been empty for a year. Running on empty is bad because it can become a habit and a lifetime. There's no urgency, once you know you can run on empty. No pressing need to put an end to the charade. This charade of living. I'm 33 33 33 33 33 33. And life has no meaning for me. It's wasted on me. There are others with an urgent drive to survive and to live to the fullest. And I don't know how to live. How do I continue?

The narcissism of Prufrock to ask, "Do I dare to disturb the universe?" No one disturbs the universe. It hovers in timeless space while we—the parade—pass by and fall over the edge of limbo. A parade on a Möbius conveyer belt, consuming itself and regurgitating new marchers. There is no different drummer. There is one drum.

Still later I wrote to a friend:

My apartment is pearl grey in the morning—mother of pearl—and bursts white at around 6:30 A.M. The leaves of my plants look sleek and oiled in the crisp light. The roses and burnished golds of the room are sweet and warm and slightly Louis XIV—a little too much; a little decadent. But the red mahogany furniture—smoldering amber in the morning sun—balances the pastels in the room.

It's a flirtatious and substantial space with my Shelleyana and poetry books—my sensuality—stacked in teak from floor to ceiling. This is my home. Any my plants grow here. My plants have what they need: sun at the start of the day and so much room in which to unfurl and unfold. I no longer starve and drown them.

I sit at my desk to write. I eat at a table. I have food in the kitchen. I have a place for everything. Everything belongs. I live in my home. I live where I live.

And yet, I feel that I am *not* blossoming or poising myself to spread my wings for flight. Rather, I feel that I am "putting my house in order," crafting a place in which to die. A place which illuminates my contours and by which I will at once be recognized and remembered.

Something inside me has changed. Something has worn out and folded in upon itself. A terrible self-hatred has been unleashed.

Last New Year's Day, I wrote to my same friend:

> Dear Sue,
> Thinking of you this New Year's. Feeling a certain sweetness that stems from knowing that I am at the beginning of the last leg of my trek back to myself. And such a sadness, too.
> This has been the best year of my life and very close to the worst. It is hard to articulate even to myself. The pain and the delight have been almost mystical—symbolic of a textbook path leading through the pain of self-knowledge and growth to the exhilaration of glimpsing this apparition of a whole self waiting for me around the corner.

Last spring, I made my version of a trek to Lourdes or Fatima: I went to the New York City Public Library to see Shelley's original manuscript of "Ode to the West Wind." Its margins had his typical doodles of trees, plus conversion equations of English pounds into lira, and lists of bills owed and things to buy. And yes, groupie to the poets that I am, I felt his presence there. I cried over the wonder that a frail, flawed human being is capable of creating godlike beauty and hope.

O wild West Wind, thou breath of Autumn's being,
Thou, from whose unseen presence the leaves dead
Are driven . . .
Be thou, Spirit, fierce,
My spirit! Be thou me, impetuous one! . . .
O, Wind,
If winter comes, can Spring be far behind?

———

**LYNN HARTNESS**

Lynn is the only person in the class I had known beforehand. I used to see her walking down Charles Street with her Walkman earphones on, and a smile that lit up an area at least from the Charles River to the top of Beacon Hill. Her Southern accent brings down-home comfort to the sometimes cool reserves of Boston. She has worked as a manager for musicians and rock groups, as an organizer of charitable fund-raising events, and is now a successful realtor. Her own paper vividly shows the powerful spirit of place that comes with a love of the land.

*The Land*

In 1941, my granddaddy, Thomas Elijiah Leigh, bought the McWhorter place. My grandmother was so happy she threw her apron over her head and cried. This farm, this land, was the culmination of all their dreams and twenty-five years of hard work. They were farmers. Every penny they had was wrested from the ground and prayed for, and the McWhorter place was the most fertile ground in the valley. They were not simple folk. They were crafty and wise. Full of humor, full of stories. They waited seven years to get married; waited for Tom to make enough money sharecropping to buy his own place. He was diligent. He worked hard. When they were twenty-eight years old, he bought a farm and they were married. My mother Grace was their only child.

In Georgia, when they got married, it was absurd to talk about or even think about being in touch with the earth. Everyone was. Land was all we had. Land was where we came from. My family emigrated from England and Scotland in the 1750s. They were farmers in Virginia, farmers in North Carolina, and in the 1840s came to Walker County, Georgia. They stayed, and are farmers there today.

I'm not sure how old I was when I first knew that land was sacred. I know from the time I could walk my mother and I would pick up papers from the side of the road. "How could strangers be so thoughtless?" I would ask. Why would anyone defile the beauty of our road? My mother's constant explanation was, "They don't own any land." I never questioned the certainty that landowners everywhere had the same standards as she. "Try to understand, Lynn; people who don't own anything cannot be expected to understand or behave as we do." I was a landowner. This land was mine, too. There was never any separation between my grandfather, my mother, and me. We owned the land. We worked the land. The Mc-Whorter place couldn't belong just to Tom. There was too much there for any one man, and I knew it was mine, too. Mine by bloodline, by birthright. I knew owning the land entailed responsibilities at an early age.

When I was ten years old, my parents had a family meeting with me and my little sister, Beth. We had an opportunity, they said, and they wanted to know what we thought. That meeting seemed natural to me. Natural that my parents would want to consult with us about an important event. "We can buy the forty-five acres that John Waters has that joins our land to the north." I looked at my father's face. He didn't own any of our land. It belonged to my mother's family, not to his. I knew how much he wanted it. I knew he wanted to be like us. I knew I'd give anything for my daddy to have what he wanted.

"That land will cost us twenty-five hundred dollars." Beth and I were stunned. Twenty-five cents a week was our pocket money and it was adequate. Twenty-five hundred dollars was a fortune. "Can we afford it?" I asked them timidly. Grace said, "We can make it if we work hard and don't have any extras. We can pay off that enormous sum in two years if we try hard. Don't make a decision yet. Let's walk the land and see if it's worth it. This means no frills for a very long time." I looked solemnly at Beth. "Let's go see it now." We probably stayed in that pasture for two hours. Picking up rocks, looking at the small stand of trees, walking the boundaries, just being out on the land.

As we walked home, I looked at Beth and she nodded. "OK. We'll do it." "This is serious business," my mother said, "but I believe it will be worth it." So did we. The next two years were spartan. My parents had never borrowed money in their lives and were panicky at being in debt. All little extras vanished, even Fritos on Friday night. But we were satisfied. We were buying land.

That acreage was always different from the rest of the farm. "John's," we called it, and our little family was different because we bought it. Beth and I learned to wait. We learned that sacrifice can bring big rewards. We learned that the most satisfaction is not necessarily in instant gratification. I learned that because we worked for and on that land.

It didn't seem strange to me that we lived on a farm, until I got to high school. I went to Center Post Elementary School and everyone there had a farm. When I was fourteen, I rode the bus to town, to high school. Most people there didn't live on farms. Their daddies worked in carpet mills or drove to Chattanooga to do mysterious white-collar jobs. Most country kids didn't excel at LaFayette High but I knew I would. I started pretending I was just like the town kids. My mother bought me Villager outfits and I was elected a class officer. I was going to college. I knew I was different, though. I didn't talk about it or worry. I just knew.

I went to college at the University of Georgia and woke up every morning with a hurt in my heart. I knew I was homesick but it took me six weeks to figure out that the pain came from missing the Blue Ridge Mountains. I felt like such a hick, but it made me smile, too. Being from a farm made me exotic and strange. I decided I liked it.

My sister and I have led very different lives. I have chosen to live for the last eight years on Beacon Hill, with the bricks and gaslights and pace of the urban east coast. Like our forefathers, Beth lives on the land. Funnily enough, she built her house on the acres we bought from John Waters. She's in touch with the land. Her husband and my mother still run the farm.

I don't live on the McWhorter place anymore, but I'm in touch with the land, too, probably in a more conscious way than the ones who came before me. Last winter I was walking in the Public Garden after the first thaw. For months, my feet had not touched the ground. I inadvertently stepped off the path and my foot felt a tingling, not unlike a mild shock. I looked down at what I could possibly be standing on and saw earth. Unfrozen, slightly muddy ground. I couldn't believe it. I was still a child of the land. It didn't matter where I was. She could reclaim me in an instant.

Many of these same memories crowded into my head at that moment. I saw my grandfather buying the farm he'd wanted all his life—finally a success at fifty-one. I saw my father buying the acres that joined my mother's—finally he belonged. I saw my sister leaving Atlanta and building a house on the place she belonged. Then I saw myself, clearly, standing on the ground. Full circle. Standing on the ground in the place that was right for me.

--------

**KAYSIE IVES**    Kaysie Ives is a tall, outdoors woman who enjoys mountain climbing and sailing. She has worked in marketing and public relations and now sells real estate in Boston. She took the course in spiritual autobiography because "a year ago my husband Gerry and I decided to have a 'year of the spirit' in which we would both look into our spiritual lives. We went to the Kripalu Center, in Lenox, Massachusetts, where we did yoga and meditation, and we read a lot in this area, and I took this course. I was worried at first that I wouldn't have time to do all the writing, but I'm happy that I managed to accomplish it." It is not surprising that Kaysie found a way to write her spiritual autobiography through telling about the sailing she loves.

*The Spirit*    Taurus is an earth sign, and I am a typical Taurus. I like the
*of Gandalf*    ease and comfort of living the good life, the sureness and safety that all is under control. But somewhere, deep in the core of my being, I sense that there should be more to life than the easy calm of the safe harbor. So I married a Capricorn and took to the sea.

We lived for four years (1974–78) on *Gandalf,* a forty-seven-foot steel sloop built in 1962 in Holland. We bought *Gandalf* from a Dutchman in St. Thomas. This meant we would have to sail up to Boston. I get butterflies in my stomach now, thinking about the anticipation of that first off-shore voyage.

But before leaving shore, we renamed the boat. *Pirana,* its former name, was too forbidding. It didn't represent the spirit of the boat. Gandalf, the wizard in *The Hobbit,* conveyed the magic of this rakish-looking boat. Gandalf, the wizard, led the hobbits into all sorts of adventures. When they invariably ran into trouble, it was Gandalf who bailed them out. He always appeared mysteriously in his green, then grey, and finally, before death, white garb. Unwittingly, we painted *Gandalf* green, then grey, then blue. He's not ready for white. He still has work to do.

Having established *Gandalf* as a spiritual entity, what's so spiritual about voyaging across oceans? In the tradition of the likes of Peter Mathiesson in *The Snow Leopard,* the physical challenge would be enough. But there is much more to adventure, as anyone who has read that book knows.

In sailing, there is a sense of awe at the vastness of your small universe as you slip along. Surrounded by the blue-green watery deep, I always feel expendable. The sea can swallow you up with one quick "glub, glub," leaving only a small ripple to tell your sad tale. At one point we sailed over the Puerto Rican Trench. Gerry remarked that you could stack forty John Hancock towers on top of each other underneath us. Twenty-six thousand feet down is equivalent to Mount Everest's height. A majestic vastness emphasized by what you see—endless water, clouds, and sky. All these pass by us in infinite variety.

Sailing journeys also have their spiritual lessons to teach. Sometimes it's hard to remember we can't cling to the present. Every time we try to grasp onto something: poof, it's gone. Not accepting the constant new games life has to offer gets us into trouble. And there is no better teacher of this lesson than the sea.

One day it's sunny and calm. Three blue dolphins swim alongside the boat, playing for hours with the lollipop I'm trailing behind. The waves easily slap the hull as we trot along. But then there's a day of flat calm. Everyone's nerves are on edge. We'll never get to Bermuda at this rate. A rhythmic slatting of the sail reminds you loudly you are going nowhere. The clouds, like statues, don't move. This is the Bermuda Triangle. This is no man's land. Then suddenly a squall hits. The boat comes to life. The sudden heeling sends dishes flying. There is disarray everywhere. Change the sails, batten down the hatches, put on foul-weather gear.

Other times, the gales go on for days. And *Gandalf* has an opportunity to work his magic and teach us another life lesson. It was a brisk thirty-five-knot northwest wind. We were coming back from Nova Scotia right into the teeth of both wind and waves. After three days of this, I was near tears, gear was breaking from the strain, and we'd been forced way south of our desired track. Suddenly, we had a brilliant breakthrough. Why fight it? We "hove to," essentially stopping forward motion. Instantly, the strain and the noise ceased. We caught some sleep, waking up to a fresh breeze which allowed us to quickly arrive in Gloucester Harbor. I wish I could learn this lesson more profoundly, but it does periodically run through my mind. Life doesn't beat you down; it's all in how you take it.

Night sailing! There's magic. Usually this is a time when you are alone on deck, steering and looking for other boats and buoys. Some nights are eerie and confined. The fog closes in, enveloping you in a damp white blanket. You know the world is out there, but you can't see twenty feet. An occasional lazy foghorn blows its warning of impending danger, or a fishing boat blasts out telling you of its presence. But for me, it is the clear, crisp, inky nights with twinkling stars that are the most magic.

One such night, while sailing over some fishing banks in the Bay of Maine, I was intently looking for other boats. The stars were luminescent, reaching down to show me the way. I sensed the intense energy of the stars, the possibility of other beings shooting magically onto the deck. Saint Exupery's Little Prince had a similar experience. I guess I actually was pretty scared, so I brought up the radio, tuned into some rock music, and turned the volume on full. The beings vanished. I came back to earth to my task of guiding *Gandalf* until the end of my watch.

Usually the stars are our friends. Because we use them to navigate, we have learned many of their names. The North Star is our guide, as the Star of Bethlehem was for the Wise Men looking for the Christ child. Orion's morning appearance tells our hearts and souls winter is coming long before we feel its chill. To know the stars are your friends is just another gift of night sailing.

Our friends the stars also give us a sense of place. How small we are! Bobbing around on one small part of a vast ocean, we dance with waves that have come from exotic lands and seas. The storm we cope with today will be another's storm tomorrow. The unpredictable is always around the corner; we learn to embrace it. The excitement and the challenge keep us alive.

Sadly, it has been two years since we sailed *Gandalf*. Gerry's and my life charts have changed. We have, by choice, other family and work challenges, other oceans to cross. We've talked about selling the boat, at the same time avoiding it. But *Gandalf* must be tired of waiting. The other night a man who saw him up on the ways, all covered with blue plastic, realized *Gandalf*'s magic. *Gandalf* could take him to Hudson Bay. We accepted his offer, heartened that *Gandalf* again will lead others on journeys of the spirit. He has sailed the Baltic, the North Sea, to Africa and Latin America, the Caribbean, the Atlantic, the Bahamas, New England, and Nova Scotia. Now he'll head north toward the Arctic. I know *Gandalf* will make it a great journey. Godspeed, *Gandalf*, on your new adventures.

———————

DENNIS DAHILL    Dennis Dahill is a program director and trainer in the Information Technologies Division of the Bank of Boston. He earned a master's degree in art education from the Rhode Island School of Design, and regularly exhibits calligraphy with the Lettering Arts Guild of Boston. Dennis is a quiet, thoughtful man of keen insight, whose deep and steady faith is apparent as he tells us his story.

*Adventure in Iran*

I've got to admit that I didn't know where to begin this autobiography until just last weekend, while I was on a group retreat in Washington, D.C. I went to the retreat looking for some direction, hoping that I might see what path to take in my life. From the start, the retreat directors asked us to spend time quietly looking for the pattern of God's action in our lives. Where and under what conditions had we experienced God working in or through us? How had coincidence (or perhaps divine intervention) shaped our destiny?

Doesn't it figure, I thought, to travel all this way asking, Where do I go from here in my life? only to find that these people want to focus on where I've been. Then again, I had gone out of my way to join this retreat, so there didn't seem to be much sense in resisting the exercises we were asked to do. Impatiently, I reviewed my life—a recollection of the times and ways in which God worked in and through and for me. And although I didn't know it at the time, I was receiving once again a precious gift: not only the "answer" to this writing assignment, but also a new context in which to appreciate the discoveries about myself and God.

By the second night, as I lay on my bed, a great comfort and peace overcame me. I hadn't gone to sleep that easily in months. All my worries about the direction my life was taking vanished and I now felt a childlike joy and a sense of certainty that I was on the right path after all. Our retreat exercises were beginning to work. Slowly I began to recall several real live interactions with God in my life—perhaps even a "divine plan" unfolding right under my nose. All I had to do was take the time to look for the signs.

Last weekend I also discovered that these experiences which constituted my relationship with God had a definite pattern, a characteristic approach that I usually take toward God and that he often takes toward me. And it was reassuring to hear that in some respects the pattern of my relationship to God was similar to the experiences of the other men and women on retreat with me.

There appear to be two ways in which I've encountered God in my life. The first is seeing how God works things out for the better even when I don't try especially hard to help him bring order out of chaos. This occurs in times of anxiety and decision: the turning points in my life when I'm quite fearful of the risks I face, but seem compelled to take them anyway.

The second experience is more direct: when, in some unexpected way, I feel God's presence in or near me. It's an odd sensation that is accompanied by an overwhelming sense of joy and wonder in everything and nothing at the same time.

One period in my life best illustrates both patterns.

About twelve years ago, I brought chaos out of order by leaving a good teaching job, my best friends, and an elegant three-bedroom apartment on Beacon Hill to attend the Rhode Island School of Design for one year. I couldn't afford professionally or financially to go to school that year, but ever since my undergraduate days in art school I had wanted to attend RISD. So when I was accepted in the art education degree program, I went with only enough money to pay for one semester's tuition and expenses. I didn't really want a degree in art education, but it came with the tuition. I studied a subject I no longer wanted to learn for the sake of the studio courses I could take to fulfill most of the degree requirements.

That year was a tremendous hardship, but also a blessing. I had to leave my apartment and move back home with my parents. This cramped my independence quite a bit, but it saved me enough money to pay an undergraduate student for the privilege of sleeping two nights a week on a lumpy studio sofa in her cold drafty loft a few blocks from the school. RISD gave me tuition assistance which kept me in school for the second semester while I cut my expenses in countless inconvenient ways. When I graduated in May, I had no job, no money and was still living at home. Returning to school seemed at that point to have been a pretty irresponsible thing to do for a little time off.

May was also far too late to apply for a job teaching art in any local school systems. Besides, I had had enough of public school teaching and I hoped to try something different. Half-heartedly I went to the school placement office to leaf through the files.

Only one teaching job appealed to me and God knows why I chose to take it seriously. An independent school in Iran was looking for a secondary school art teacher. Where was Iran? I wasn't even sure how to pronounce it. For some reason I followed up on the lead. I went home to find a map and to compose my résumé. A week or so after writing to the school, I interviewed with the headmaster who, coincidentally, was attending a conference in New Hampshire.

A few weeks later, I was offered a two-year contract and had all of fifteen days to pack my bags, get my passport, shots, etc. I even took the train to New York to get a visa because I feared the post office might lose my passport. In mid-August I left family and friends behind. Perhaps it was the right time in my life to leave home, but I had so much to do I didn't think much about why I was going.

I had never traveled alone before. My flight from Boston to Tehran included a one-day stopover in London. After landing at Heathrow, I took a taxi to the only address I knew in London, a retreat house run by an order of priests who staffed my parish church back home. I had stayed with them for a few nights on my first visit to London six years earlier on a vacation with two friends from college.

Jim, my best friend in college, had joined that order and was studying in London. I had hoped to see him and perhaps spend a night in that huge brick rectory. The guest master, who told me Jim was in Oxford that week, seemed a bit embarrassed by the mix-up. He waited for me to say goodbye, but I figured I might at least ask for a room for the night. It took a little courage for me to be so bold, but I was offered a room with a view of Westminster Abbey, the last sight of civilization I expected to see for quite some time.

To celebrate my budding independence, I attended evensong in the abbey. I always go there whenever I'm in London. It's a point of reference for me, a place where I can leave my concerns outside, collect my thoughts, and pray for rest and refreshment in a place that's warm and familiar. As I sat in the choir with its gilt stalls and singing choirboys, I wondered if I would even see a church for the next two years.

The next day I flew to Tehran. A young man with a shaved head and tattered coat sat next to me. He was going on to India to study a form of meditation with some Hindu guru or other. I thought he was a bit misguided, until I looked out the window as we approached the runway in Tehran.

Sand. Brown sand for as far as the eye could see. And real hovels—not the romantic "hovel" I used to joke about living in on Beacon Hill. My friend said to me, "Are you sure you want to get off here?" It seemed we each thought the other was crazy.

Why was I in Iran? I had no clear idea. Certainly not for the very small salary I was to earn at the school. I wasn't even the adventurous type!

After an all-night welcome party in the headmaster's house, a fellow teacher walked me through the dark alleys near the school to his apartment, where I fell asleep on a foam mattress spread out on the roof.

During the night, I heard a man chanting from the Koran—a whining melody that echoed through my jet-lagged brain like a distant dream. But I knew it wasn't a dream; it was coming from a house among hundreds that surrounded this rooftop dormitory. In the morning, I woke to the sound of cooing doves and a blinding, hot sun.

My Iranian adventure had begun. It would be full of stories, but one stands out as my most immediate experience of God.

All of the veteran teachers told us new arrivals the most exciting stories of beautiful mountain pastures, little streams, and happy encounters with the nomads. So one autumn day, a dozen teachers and I planned a mountain climbing expedition. It was really just a day trip out of the city. The clean air would do us all good.

The day of the trip, I packed my bag with a couple of sandwiches, a bottle of wine and some drinking water, my sketch pad, and a box of watercolors. (As an art teacher, I thought it important to set a good example for my students by bringing back some of my own sketches to show in class the following week.)

Our leader on this excursion was the high school French teacher, Gertrude, a licensed Swiss mountain guide and giver of good advice about safety as well as admonitions for being late. Gertrude was on the verge of telling the bus driver to leave without me, as I ran down the street toward the mini-bus waving my sketch pad to catch her attention, and trying to keep my loosely packed flight bag from slipping off my shoulder while I ran.

It was early morning and already getting hot, and I vowed never to speak to Gertrude again if she left me behind in a cloud of dust. When I reached the bus I realized that her boss, the high school principal, was running about fifty paces behind me. (Had I known this I would have walked!)

We rode about fifty miles out of Tehran and up a gently sloping mountain to a mine shaft at about six thousand feet. The ride up the extremely narrow road is a hair-raising story for another time. Suffice it to say that everyone's prayers were answered. The driver parked the bus beside an apple orchard and we began our climb up a dusty trail.

At first, I stopped every now and then to observe the view. The trail was not steep and we climbed as a group for most of the morning, stopping for lunch beside a grassy cow pasture.

After lunch, I climbed in earnest and went on ahead of the others. Near the top of the peak was an outcropping, a little rocky ledge that I set as my goal for the day's climb. From that moment on I avoided looking back toward the view. I knew a spectacular landscape stretched out behind me and I wanted to be swept off my feet when I reached the top and took it all in at once! I climbed with real purpose and growing anticipation.

Soon enough, I reached that ledge. It was much larger than I expected. I grabbed its sandy ridge as I crawled up on top, fixing my gaze all the while on the dark reddish-brown rock under my hands and feet.

I set my feet firmly on the ledge and slowly turned around.
The height made me dizzy and I dared not take a step.
Blue hills, violet horizon, cloudless blue sky.
Brown-grey sand and red rock.

I felt the atmosphere wrap around me like a blanket—like a cloud. A warm gentle breeze covered me. God himself was caressing me in the wind! My heart was pounding, not from the climb but from the thrill of an encounter with unimaginable beauty. I inhaled the gentle breeze, filling my lungs with the awesome spirit of God. Creation and I were one.

I thought that if I could fly I'd leap from my ledge, dive into the deep green valleys far below, swim in the violet sea of those distant hills. I was dazzled by the light of the sun and the motion of the hills that spread out like waves of blue and violet under that thin blue sky.

I remembered the Psalm: "The mountains skipped like rams, the hills like the lambs of the flock."

Indeed they do.
Strong solid mountains with deep vivid colors.
But gentle spiritual wind, all soft and light and warm.
For just a few minutes, I stood there alone with God.
Was that the reason for my journey to Iran?

O how I love you my God,
    for giving me such pleasure!
For knowing what I need and when I need it.
You are sublime like the mountain,
    like the mighty peaks wrapped in gentle warm
    breezes.
You are greater than anything I have ever seen—
    too wonderful to be imagined!
Is this why the Moslems don't even try to depict you?
Surely, it is—I tried.

Sitting on my mountaintop, I opened my watercolor box and began to splash the pale earthy tones across a 12″ × 18″ sheet of white paper.

How futile.

My exhilaration turned to frustration and pain. My joy was in the encounter with incredible beauty and, yes, with God himself, and yet I felt pain in the sorrow of not understanding how to express the joy, how to capture the beauty, how to understand the mystery of the encounter. How weakly I responded—so inarticulate in the face of a great communication of spirit and matter. God and me. I felt a joyful sadness in my heart.

My drawings didn't turn out very well. I took them home and tacked them to the wall in my bedroom. The only time they looked appealing was in the half-light of early morning. An hour later, they were ugly again. Yet for an hour a day, in dim light, those curious paintings repeat a simple theme: the beauty of God's subtlety and the inadequacy of human understanding. They suggest the experience of an encounter with majesty but do not, cannot, duplicate it.

Those paintings, perhaps like the breeze on that mountaintop, inspire only me. They fill my heart with a recollection of the One I met that day. And like the pale light of dawn, they softly illuminate my imagination, coaxing it to give up its subtle revelations, its secrets—hidden in the heart and expressed only as an impression.

I left Iran a little more than a year later, as the most recent revolution was getting under way. All my doubts about the wisdom of going to that country were reawakened. In the midst of street fighting, martial law, and strikes, I asked myself if this terror was what I came to the Middle East for. Gone for the moment was the memory of my solitary encounter with the author of creation. I became a confused and needy child that wanted to go home.

I was sharing an apartment that year with my friend John, who taught in our elementary school. One night, an hour or so after the curfew, a particularly noisy and dangerous demonstration broke out just a few blocks from our apartment. The troops were shooting into a large crowd of people who had rallied in a nearby square. We decided that the time had come to leave Tehran.

As I lay on my bed in my darkened room, I heard the

neighbors shouting from their rooftops, "Allah Akbar!"—God is great! I wondered, were they angry with us, the American teachers who lived in their midst? That night, I doubted I would be able to leave Iran before something dreadful happened to me or to my friends. In desperation I prayed to God, "Get me out of here!"

The next morning, John and I began what we thought was a sensibly planned departure. We packed our bags, bought plane tickets, and tried twice to leave, but there was always a problem—with the tickets, with the visas, with customs, and so on. So we stayed on for a couple of days, hoping for the best.

Within a few days and in spite of overwhelming incompetence on the part of the police and customs officials, John and I were the first two teachers from our school to leave Tehran. As far as I know, all of the other teachers were able to depart safely as well. With the help of the parents of one of John's students, we even got our trunks through customs, a good fortune some of our colleagues did not share.

We stopped in London on our way home. While John went out on his own late one afternoon I returned to the gilded choir stalls of Westminster Abbey to listen to evensong.

It was mid-December, about a week before Christmas. I looked up at the Gothic arches, a Moslem invention brought to Europe by medieval traders, and thought how coincidental it was that I should find myself sitting in this holy place whenever I had something to be thankful for. "Thank you, Father," I prayed, "for bringing me safely to this place again."

———

**MARIA S. JUDGE**   Maria is the assistant dean for the Fletcher School of Law and Diplomacy at Tufts University. She writes that she "spends her days keeping the school safe from financial imbalances, and her evenings keeping the world safe from social imbalances. In her spare time, she wonders why she has so little spare time." We at the Boston Center who have come to know Maria count the time she spends with us a delightful gift. She has traveled extensively in both outer and inner ways.

*Pilgrimage*    I don't know if my mother and father talked about God on their first date, but they met through the Newman Club, so there's a good chance that he may have entered the conversation. There is a great deal that I don't know about my parents, and the years have dulled rather than piqued my curiosity. But no matter how they ended up, I do know that they started out together as very Good Catholics. A Jesuit who had been one of my mother's professors at Boston College told me once that back in her student days he used to ask her occasionally if she had found that special someone, and she would tell him not yet, but that she wasn't worried because God would provide. In the middle of the wedding ceremony at which he officiated, she pointed to her new husband and whispered to Father Leonard, "See, God did provide." I have often thought that he must not be such a terrific provider if that was the best he could do.

There was a great deal of water in my life map, little blue squiggles representing the oceans I crossed in my life. I made my first journey *in utero*. My mother was pregnant with me when they crossed the Channel to go from Ireland to Germany, where I was born a few months later. My parents had lived in Ireland for about three years, having left their hometown of Boston shortly after their marriage to study in Dublin, a popular thing to do in the postwar era. Their first child was born the following year and died a few days later of heart problems. We always knew about Joseph, and my mother would often mention him in July, on his birthday. "Well, Joseph would have been sixteen today." There was never any sense of sadness or regret when she mentioned him, so I never thought of his death as a tragic event. I used to wonder what it would have been like if he had lived. Surely he would have been a better big brother than Andrew, who was born a year later, and did his share of picking on me. I thought that even if Joseph wouldn't have stuck up for me, he at least would have picked on Andrew, who would then have known what it was like to suffer such torment.

As true Good Catholics my parents followed the fine tradition of naming their children after the saint on whose feast day they were born. I happened to arrive on the feast of Pope Pius V, and since in my early years I had something of a bed wetting problem, I considered myself fortunate that they did not carry through this ritual with me. "Pia" would have been too much to handle. Since nine more children followed closely after Joseph, and we all were given at least two names, they had ample opportunity to cover almost two dozen of the heavenly hosts. Many years later I asked my mother why they had decided to have so many children. She said, "Well, we just thought that God would provide," and shrugged as if to say, "I guess we were a little naive." I think she had long ago realized that God often needed help and that they hadn't always met him halfway.

When I was about six months old we went back to Ireland for another year and then returned to the United States. We settled in Indiana for several years, long enough for four more little saints to arrive. After having had the first two children in different countries, Brigid, Cecelia, Robert, and Valentina (guess when she was born!) were all delivered by the same doctor at the same hospital. We moved at least three more times during this five-year period, in and out of houses and neighborhoods. I started school with the terrifying nuns, and at home I became mother's little helper, standing on stools to reach the sink to do dishes, and assuming responsibility for two or three younger ones.

One day when I was seven, we were told that we were going to visit our grandparents in Boston. There was a great deal of packing and planning, and we hopped a train and wound up in a hotel where I could look out the window and see the Statue of Liberty. We were in Hoboken, and at that point we were told that we were going to Ireland, not Boston.

I felt betrayed. My parents had lied, and I think in many ways I began to distrust them from that moment on. We spent a somewhat mixed-up year in Ireland, living in the same house in the Wicklow Hills where my parents had lived on their previous Irish sojourn. Ten years before they had rented rooms in the guest house at Valclusa; this time we had the whole house to ourselves. There are good memories of that year, of playing at the Powerscourt Waterfall, of herding and milking the cows, of visits by the tinkers, and of the acres of gorgeous countryside for our playground. But it was also a confusing time. We went to a small, three-room schoolhouse that was several miles away. We frequently had to walk since the only transportation was the local postman, who used to drop us off on his way to work. We were part novelty—the American kids—and part freaks, and adjusting was difficult. After I had been in school for a few weeks, I was caned by the second-grade teacher (the master), when my seatmate accidentally smudged my copybook before I'd had a chance to blot it. In my mind's version of the incident I fled home that day in tears, and when my father found out what had happened, he went in and confronted the master, demanding an apology and a promise never to hit me again. But in reality I had apparently come home sobbing and refused to say what had happened. Somehow I had already picked up enough weird vibes to not say very much about anything and to handle all my problems myself.

We returned to Indiana, long enough for the arrival of Justin and my settling in to third grade, only to be uprooted a few months later by the move to Chile. We spent three years there. Since it was the longest period I remembered spending anywhere, I found myself settling into the routine there. I went to a small school (two rooms this time) where no one spoke English, so I learned Spanish before anyone else in the family. My mother was still walking around with a dictionary in hand, while I conversed fluently. The pattern that I was developing began to perfect itself. I adapted well and coped quietly.

Then, of course, it was time to leave again, and we packed up and came back to the States, and settled in a small town south of Boston. I hated this move more than any of the others. Everything was foreign here. We were supposed to have come home, but I didn't feel like I had a home anymore. I was teased at school for doing things differently. I even set up division problems Chilean-style, which other kids thought was very strange. One of my grandmothers died just after we got back and the other one was a little strange. She used to come visit, and would tell me things that worried me terribly. She couldn't understand why my father felt he had to try to save the world and drag his family with him. Why couldn't he settle down and buy a home and support his family properly, the way his older brother had? Of course, my own thoughts had also run somewhat along this line. Why did we have to keep moving so often? The strange thing was that my grandmother's dissatisfaction with her middle son was the only negative voice to be heard. Everybody else thought we had a wonderful life. "What a wonderful opportunity you children had!" we were always being told. "Weren't you lucky to go all those wonderful places?" This was not my idea of luck, but since I heard it from just about every adult we ever met, I soon decided I was an ungrateful child to feel so miserable about the friends and places I would never see again.

My family had always been regular churchgoers and my father was even a lector at Mass when we first came back to the States. But I don't remember any particular sense of spirituality about church, or about our lives for that matter, and I suspect that my parents found it increasingly difficult to practice what they preached. Eventually we all drifted away.

My father began to get stranger over the next few years. One of his little routines was to call regular family meetings where he would carry on about finances, the household, the family, and so on. There never seemed to be any point to these sessions, but I was always reduced to tears of frustration and anger, frustrated that I didn't know what he wanted, and angry that he was laying such a guilt trip on his children. The summer I was fourteen was the worst. These meetings often took place just before I had to go to work, and after we had adjourned and I had mopped myself up, he would drive me to work as though nothing had happened. I was furious that my mother never stood up for us, but I guess she was as miserable as the rest of us. When I found her crying I would feel so helpless. Years later I found out that my father had lost a job and that the trip to Ireland was not a sabbatical, as I had always thought, but a place he fled to while he tried to regroup. And the Peace Corps was not an act of Christian charity, but rather the best thing waiting for him when he came back after his year away. He was simply a man who could not cope with any kind of failure, particularly the kinds he brought on himself, and as life got tougher, he somehow needed to include everyone else in his misery.

After the eighth grade I got tired of being different, so I learned how to blend in and become one of the crowd. Eventually I found that I had submerged my identity so well that I had no idea who I was.

My college years were spent with the Jesuits, in a school that was grappling with its religious identity. There seemed to be a lot of questioning about whether or not it was still a Catholic college. I had no interest in the answer. I think there was a part of me that was searching for something, and that led me to try a retreat, and to try working with the liturgical committee to plan a Mass or two. But I never seemed to find any answers, and finally even forgot what my questions were.

I spent my junior year in Madrid, enjoying life away from everything I had known before. On a visit to the northern part of the country one of the hotels where we stayed had a single room and, since everyone else wanted a roommate, I took it for the night. I realized, at age twenty-one, that it was the first time in my life I had ever had a room to myself. Over Christmas break I had a chance to visit Germany and Ireland. It was a strange and exciting experience to revisit places where I had lived so long ago. I went to the old schoolhouse in Kilmacanogue and to Christmas Eve midnight Mass at the church near Waterloo Road where my parents had gone so many years before. I recall with a sense of spiritual wonder the feeling I had walking up Rathnaustrasse in Hamburg, holding my breath in the hope that the house I was born in would still be there.

The following month my roommate and I decided to do some weekend traveling to use up our Eurail passes. For some reason I had always wanted to visit Lourdes and Fatima, and we decided to go to both places. Our friends thought they were slightly odd choices, and we were very casual about it. "Oh yes," we would say, "it's Lourdes this weekend, Fatima the next, and the following week we're joining the convent." At Fatima, way out in the country, removed from everything and everyone, sitting in the spot where the children had seen the Virgin so many years before, I felt such a sense of peace and possibility that I would not have been surprised to see a vision myself.

The next few years were busy. I tried to get on with my life. After graduation, I worked uncertainly for a few years, went back to graduate school, and then worked unhappily for another year or so, wondering what to do with my life. Before, I had always operated in the short term. No matter how bad things got, I only had to last until the next move. I could leave the country, or leave school, or leave a job, or go back to school. There was always a way out. Now there were no more moves on the agenda, and I felt lost when forced to face the long term. But then I took a new job where I somehow began to feel as though all my disjointed parts were at last coming together. I think in many ways I found a place where I could belong, where I was productive and hardworking and terribly clever and much appreciated—everything I had never quite been before. It felt like home, and I felt as though I were in control. My outer life now seemed full, but I began to feel an inexplicable emptiness inside. I went to talk to the campus chaplain around Thanksgiving time, thinking that perhaps some volunteer work might fill this void which I could not identify. But another opportunity presented itself instead.

My return journey really got underway with the help of the Sanctuary Movement and Thomas Merton. I heard of the first a week or so after my Thanksgiving meeting with the chaplain, on 2 December 1984. It was the fourth anniversary of the slaying of four North American churchwomen in El Salvador. At a service that evening, the new university chaplain talked about how churches in this country were becoming sanctuaries to help Central Americans who had fled their countries. He announced that a campus committee would be formed to see what action could be taken at the university, and I just knew that this was for me. I went to the first meeting and became very active over the next few years, first on campus, and then in Somerville and throughout Boston. I also became very close to the chaplain, which was an interesting experience for me, since my only prior models for religious people had been priests and nuns. This man was very different. He was a Unitarian minister, married with two children, a warm, involved, caring person who was somehow able to strike a balance between spirituality and everyday life. I found I could relate to him not only as a minister, but also as a human being and colleague. He also got me involved in chaplaincy activities and a few months after we met he invited me to speak at the Good Friday celebration of the Seven Last Works of Christ. I was flattered that he thought me "religious" enough to have something to contribute, though I couldn't imagine what I would talk about.

Sanctuary's most important role was in making me aware of the spiritual void in my life. During the course of research for a paper I was writing, I interviewed two refugees in sanctuary, a Guatemalan man at the Community Church of Boston, and a Salvadoran woman at the Old Cambridge Baptist Church, along with members of each congregation. I was awed by the sense of community I found in each place and by the direction in which their faith had led these people. It gave me a whole new outlook on faith, and I found myself envying the people who could work together so well. I found myself wanting to be able to feel that way, too.

I came across Merton almost by accident, idly flipping TV channels one night. I stopped at PBS and sat there for the next hour watching a fascinating documentary on his life. I found him so intriguing that I felt an actual sense of loss when I learned that he had died seventeen years before. I began to read his works, as well as those of his biographers, made three trips to Gethsemane, the abbey in Kentucky where he spent his entire monastic life, and found myself very caught up in his life. I'm still not entirely sure why he appealed to me so much, but it probably had to do with some similar patterns in our early lives, the moves, the sense of isolation, and the desire to belong somewhere. I think I was also ready for something, and his story was so fascinating and instructive. The hellbent secular life did not fulfill him. He found his niche in the spiritual self, and found the world by retreating to a monastery. I had no intention of joining the cloister myself, but I felt more and more that I was being moved along a path with some meaning.

In January 1987 I began to go to church again, first as part of a New Year's resolution, later because I wanted to. I had tried a few services outside the Catholic church, but they hadn't felt quite right and the Paulist Center did. They were concerned about hunger and homelessness and Central America and lost souls, and seemed to have moved far beyond the kind of church that had so little meaning for me years before.

I think it was the sense of belonging I found there that made me ready for Nicaragua. I had been involved in Central American issues for several years, and felt that it was time for me to go there and see for myself what was happening. And Nicaragua intrigued me. I had written a paper the previous year on the role of the Catholic church there. Ernesto Cardenal, the Nicaraguan poet, priest, and minister of culture, had once been a monk at Gethsemane, when Merton was novice master there, and Merton had hoped to go to Nicaragua to found a monastic community. He never did, but I thought perhaps I could make my pilgrimage there.

It was indeed a pilgrimage, and went far beyond anything I expected. I felt very much that I was under the control of a higher power, that God was with me the whole time. I traveled with Witness for Peace, a faith-based group operating on the belief that those who work for peace must be willing to take the same risks as those who fight in wars. Accordingly, WFP delegations travel to war zones to be with the people whose lives have been uprooted by the seemingly endless war. Each member of the delegation takes a vow of nonviolence, and as I took mine I thought of the three great peacekeepers in the world—Christ, Gandhi and Martin Luther King—whose nonviolent approaches had moved mountains. I also thought of how each of them died a violent death, and

I wondered what I would do if I were to be faced with death on this trip.

On the final leg of our journey into northern Nicaragua, we were to travel by open truck some twenty-five miles from Jinotega City to Yali, a small village about thirty miles from the Honduran border, in the heart of the war zone. As we waited in the morning for the truck to arrive, we were notified that there was contra activity on the road. The government gave us permission to proceed, but wanted us to be aware of the risks. Driving over bumpy, winding roads, we sang songs, hymns, show tunes, and even Elvis Presley, until my throat was raw. It was a mystical experience to be riding in that desolate area, not really knowing if the truck would be attacked or not, but somehow feeling safe and protected and never alone. I remember looking up into the mountains and thinking of the passage from Psalms about lifting my eyes up unto the hills from where cometh my strength. I felt that I was living that passage.

On our first morning in the village we were awakened at five-thirty in the morning by the sound of heavy artillery fire, and soon were informed that a contra attack had taken place in a resettlement camp a few miles away. At noon our delegation held a silent vigil in the town square and the villagers joined us. A tiny, ancient woman slipped into the circle next to me and held my hand, asking who we were and when we had come. I told her about Witness for Peace and she said to me, "We have been praying to God for help and you have come in answer to our prayers." I had never been an answer to anyone's prayers before, and I felt honored and humbled that she chose me to hear these words.

That evening as we prepared to visit with the family in whose tiny shack three of us were staying, the lights suddenly went out and a bell began ringing in the street outside. Our hostess told us that the nearby power station had been blown up by the contras. The ringing bell indicated that the town was on full alert, since the darkness increased the likelihood of a direct attack. We could go to bed if we wanted, she said, but we should sleep in our clothes and keep shoes and flashlights nearby in case we had to get to a safer house in the middle of the night.

After we had been in bed for about ten minutes, I realized I had forgotten to light my candle that evening. At our commissioning service, one of the speakers suggested that those who waited for us at home light a candle each evening to pray for us. I had lit a candle every evening while I wrote in my journal, but tonight had overlooked the ritual. I hesitated, but tonight of all nights it seemed too important to miss. I climbed out of bed, located the candle in the bottom of my bag, lit it, and then sat on the end of the bed. Jann, Pam, and I talked quietly in the candle's glow, and a sense of peace settled over me. The words of the song we had sung in the morning came back to me: "Be not afraid, I go before you always. Come, follow me, and I will give you strength." I blew out the candle and went to sleep.

As I write this, I am aware of what a significant date it is. Forty-seven years ago today, on 10 December 1941, Thomas Merton entered the Monastery of Our Lady of Gethsemane. Forty years ago today, 10 December 1948, the Universal Declaration of Human Rights was signed in Paris. And twenty years ago today, 10 December 1968, Merton died in an accident in Thailand. His life was divided in half: twenty-seven years outside the walls, and twenty-seven years inside. Most of us don't have such clear divisions in our lives, and I cannot divide mine into stages with such specific boundaries. Things seem to flow into each other in a pattern that I can only assume will one day make sense.

Merton wrote, "In one sense we are always traveling and traveling as if we did not know where we were going. In another sense we have already arrived." My journey, of course, was ordained long before I arrived to begin it. We are all products of those who go before us, and just as my early road was paved by my parents' actions, so were their roads paved by their parents. But regardless of the miles of ancestral journeys that flow through my veins, I know that lately I have traveled farther inside myself than I ever traveled in my wandering childhood years.

———

SELINA
KASSELS

Selina Kassels is a clinical psychologist who, in her own words, "designs and supervises programs in behavioral medicine and has a private practice in psychotherapy. Her home overlooks the Boston skyline with its ever-changing lights, sunrises and sunsets." She is a thoughtful, caring person who volunteered to observe my first intensive two-day workshop at Interface, to advise me how to handle any psychological problems arising from the intensity of this kind of writing in such a short space of time. In fact, no such problems surfaced, but Selina's presence at my first experience in leading the two-day course was reassuring.

*On the
Journey*

"Life is a journey, not a destination." I read that quote this summer. I don't remember where, or who the author was. I saw it in passing as I was browsing through some resources while preparing a talk on stress management.

The words stuck with me. When I think back over my life in terms of destinations, I often feel a sense of loss and personal failure. The sense of loss arises when I think of the contrast between destinations I had hoped to arrive at and places where I wound up. Usually my destinations are the places I thought I *should* be, the marriage and career goals that mark "success" in our society. As soon as I change my focus—thinking of my life in terms of a journey—I'm often astonished at where I've been and feel blessed at the opportunities and experiences I've had.

Looking back, it feels as if my planned destinations have not been as important as the detours I took along the road. The best of my life has been lived along the detours. The unexpected places at which I've arrived have changed my future destinations. Only when I'm looking back does it feel as if I was meant to arrive at that detour—and that the process of the journey was truly the most important destination.

After graduating from college, I wanted to get away. It was hard for me to imagine settling down then, although that was what everyone else was doing. Finding a husband was the purpose of women going to college, then. Most of my friends married soon after graduation and found themselves in suburban homes that were so easy to buy, then. I wanted more.

More meant seeing the world. My first trip to Israel in the summer of 1969 started out as a "detour." I had by then already traveled to many places of my dreams—to Europe, to Mexico and to California. Deciding to go to Israel was not much of a decision. Summer was coming. I was alone again, recovering from the breakup of a long-term relationship, looking for adventure and romance. Israel popped into my mind.

Israel had been the place they always talked about in Hebrew school, a new state carved out of the desert. Planting a tree in Israel was a ritual of my youth, like selling Girl Scout cookies. When I was a college student and young adult, Israel had never been a focus of my concern. Not until June of 1967. Then Israel flashed into all of our lives: a living myth of David slaying Goliath. Israel became fashionable and chic with intellectuals, not only with Jews, so it just popped into my mind as a place I'd like to go for vacation.

My trip to Israel turned out to be far more than a Club Mediterranean vacation (although it was that, as well). I went to Israel alone, not knowing anyone there. As soon as our El Al flight landed at Lod Airport, I felt strangely at home, surrounded by "family." This was a feeling that grew stronger each day I spent in Israel, and each time I visited, which I did for three out of the four following summers.

Falling in love with a country sounds trite. But that is what I experienced about Israel. And this love affair opened my heart to my deeper roots: to my identity as a Jew.

Israel was the first place where I had ever heard Hebrew spoken in lyrical tones. It was a different language than the harsh guttural sounds spoken by the aging, pitiful Hebrew school teacher with his potbelly and suspenders. There was a lilting quality to the language spoken by my new friends, Yaira and Rami. Hebrew was used to banter on the beaches of Tel Aviv. It was the language used by the Israeli cast in their version of the hit musical *Hair.* It was a living language.

I had never read or studied the Bible beyond the obligatory passages I stumbled through in Hebrew school. Now the Bible also became alive. Standing in the Jerusalem Hills, watching the setting sun flash on the golden Dome of the Rock, and seeing the Judean desert stretching endlessly to the east I felt that this was a special place, a city meant to inspire and nurture civilizations. It became important for me to read and hear stories about the Bible; important to hear stories of the destruction and rebuilding of our temples; stories of the birth and life of Jesus; as well as stories of the newer religion of Islam that had come to claim this city as its own.

My heart also opened to the stories of the history of my people, their wanderings. As a child I had brushed aside the stories of my immigrant grandparents and breathed a sigh of relief when we left their noisy, Yiddish-speaking house in the ghetto, returning to our quiet tree-lined streets and home. In Israel, I relished hearing the accents of Eastern Europe in the marketplaces and smiled at shopkeepers who called me a *shayna madela* [pretty young woman]. In a secondhand bookshop, the owner invited me for tea, and told me his story. I was drawn to his eyes—the same blue eyes, the Russian eyes that reminded me of my father. This man had immigrated to Palestine from Russia shortly after the Revolution. I listened to the details.

When I returned to Boston, I sought out my aunts for the first time to learn about my own roots. I heard the details. My father had been detained on Ellis Island, a stowaway who escaped being arrested and sent to Siberia. I heard about an aunt who had as a little girl survived a pogrom while witnessing the murder of a pregnant woman. She lived with the memory of seeing soldiers slash open the womb. She lived with the memory of seeing the fetus. A vacation trip to Israel opened many chapters for me.

I never would have imagined myself climbing a mountain. But I did climb one. In August 1973, I climbed Mount Sinai. As strange as it may seem, I still was not aware of searching for a religious experience at Mount Sinai, just for an experience. I had grown to love the summer vacations I spent in Israel, with sun, shopping, adventure, and romance: good vacations. I was drawn back to friends I had made, and had some thoughts of emigrating. A tour to the desert promised more adventure.

It was adventurous. A van carried our tour group across the white sand plains of the northern Sinai. The barren horizon seemed like a moonscape. The remains of rusting and deserted tanks were the only signs of life. The tanks were the unplanned memorials to the battles that had expanded Israel's frontiers. They were also used for "pit stops"; men went on one side of the van and women on the other.

We stayed up the first night in the humid, hot air of camp on the Gulf of Suez. By the second night, we had arrived at the Santa Katerina Monastery at the base of Mount Sinai. Awakened at 3:00 A.M., we gathered in a procession behind the Bedouins and camels to begin our hike under the stars.

As we climbed, the sun started to rise, gradually bathing the surrounding mountains in a pale light. At first I was amazed mostly at the miracle that I was continuing to push on. Our group consisted mostly of young tourists from France and England who were used to hiking and ready to tease this soft American. As the sun continued to rise, I forgot all about my wobbly legs.

By 6:00 A.M. we reached the summit. The sun shone over the jagged peaks of the whole sandstone range of the Sinai Mountains. I remember staring at the sunrise and vaguely hearing the group of young Israelis chanting morning prayers as they put on Tefillin. This place seemed very close to God.

Looking back, I will never forget that sunrise. It was the first time I "took in" the sunrise, and it became part of me. I came closer to Judaism, but did not go to live in Israel. My heart stayed there for a long time. I was here in Boston weeks later when sirens shattered the silence of Yom Kippur. My friends, my "brothers," were called from their prayers to defend their borders. Some of my friends, some of my "brothers," were changed by that war. I was changed. We were changed. It became hard to go back.

I never expected to tire of traveling. But I did. I came to realize that I was traveling not to visit places, but to open up inner spaces. Traveling to leave behind the routines of my daily life and to find peak experiences. Israel had opened the doors to new paths. The first time I found myself writing a poem was on the plane, on my first return trip to Israel.

Later I learned that I could find the poetry closer to home, that I could go on trips here, too. And that wherever and whenever I took time to look at the sky, I could find the mystery and adventure I had found in Israel.

———

LISE BEANE

The remarkable evening that began with the paper by Jana which I feared would intimidate all the others ended just as remarkably with this contribution by Lise Beane. Lise is a clear-talking, no-nonsense sort of woman who works as a free-lance advertising copywriter. I have come to know her as a person of great creative imagination and wide-ranging interests, who hostessed many of our follow-up meetings at her apartment. She later led a course at the Boston Center called "Planning the Perfect Trip through the English Countryside." That evening of the class I was moved by the power and depth of her spiritual autobiography.

*A Christmas Story*

I have a small, double-sided mirror on my vanity, on which I have pasted two small quotes, one on each side. The first quote reads, "The human spirit is stronger than anything that can happen to it." The second quote reads, "Only one who can see the invisible can do the impossible." Every morning when I put on my makeup, I look at these two quotes. The first quote gives me a sense of security. The second quote, a sense of wonder.

Love, security, and wonder have always been essential ingredients in my life. I bring all three of these properties together when I create.

A few years ago, as a hobby, I started teaching children to create. I did it out of a sense of love and wonder. I had just reread Rollo May's exciting book, *The Courage to Create,* and I was eager to incorporate what I had learned. I made a game out of learning to invent toys and stories, and played it with the kids. With the children's easy access into the world of imagination, we were off and creating in no time.

Together, we discovered Funus, the tenth planet of the solar system, the only natural health-spa planet in the universe created exclusively for kids. Together, we invented Night Flyer sleds and coordinated Captain Midnight helmets that light up in the dark, so the kids could sled past dusk. Together, we developed the first camcorder script kits, so we could film our own movies. Movies with titles such as, *Escape from Gorilla Island, Eeek, Meet My Family, My Room: A Disaster Area* and the ever-popular classic, *Gone with My Mind.* Together, we invented windup Penguin Pens that waddle across your desk, then stop to rest alongside jagged Glacier Erasers. Together, we designed hot-dog-shaped novelty food items made of cream-puff rolls, ice-cream hot dogs and chocolate-sauce mustard.

Together, we have created an entire, professional-quality portfolio of totally original toys and stories. And together we have had hours of fun and happiness.

I have a theory that when we create, our bodies produce a natural chemical that makes us happy. The chemical helps to encourage and sustain us through the creative process. I know that our bodies produce morphine-like endorphins to see us through strenuous physical exercise. I believe the same holds true for periods of great creative activity. The reason for this is that creativity is essential to mankind.

I do not know how I create. The end result of the process is not mine to explain, but I do know how I begin. I start by having an intense involvement with a subject. Then, as a helpful exaggeration, I imagine myself walking up a few steps in my mind and sitting at my computer. My computer is my brain and its screen is my mind's eye. I work hard at my computer, feeding in every question I can possibly think of that I want to know about that given subject. After that, I feed in all information pertinent to that subject as it comes in. Additionally, I put in a call to my memory to bring forth any and all information I may have stored on that subject in the past. Then I go into a state of deep relaxation, and wait. Inevitably, my brain gives me the answer to the problems I have put to it, most often upon awakening in the morning.

Recently, I told a teacher friend of mine in London about this process. She said, yes, that many people used to do this before they invented television. It was called "thinking." We both laughed about this, but I know the difference between thinking and creating. Thinking you do for yourself; creating your brain does for you.

Creating has become very important for me. As I have gotten older, many of life's problems have not gotten any easier for me. As a matter of fact, many of them have gotten harder.

For example, for the last two years, my family and I helped nurse my youngest brother, aged twenty-eight, through a series of debilitating illnesses, all the while knowing there was no cure for what he had. The experience was excruciating for all of us, and toward the end, it was akin to watching Christ die on the cross every day for about two months straight.

During this time, I felt the need to find a spiritual understanding of death I could use to see me through not only this death, but future deaths sure to follow, including, eventually, my own. I have wrestled this question of spirituality and death all over the globe. And in the end, I have had to make myself see beyond the you and me in this room right now, to try to understand the possibilities for all of us tomorrow.

I believe that, because of my need to find this information, my brain created some thoughts for me. Two pieces of what may be parts of some gigantic puzzle were given to me, fait accompli, on separate occasions. A religious person would perhaps call these two foreign ideas that popped into my head "revelations." Not being a religious person, I took them to mean I needed a long vacation, and took one. But when I came back from the vacation, I took out these two strange ideas again, and played with them, examining them from every angle.

Here is the first idea:

Your subconscious, conscious and superconscious are a microcosm of hell, earth, and heaven.

About two weeks later, the second idea popped into my

head almost as though it were trying to clarify the first idea. It is:

Heaven is the creative energy source for the future of mankind.

I invite any and all interpretations of these two thoughts, but in the meantime, this is what I have come to think they mean.

When we die, our spirits go home to heaven. But in actuality, it is our divine creative energy which goes home to its source: an energy source that has existed since the beginning of time. This great eternal energy source renews itself like rain. Parts of it are sent forth to be used, and then returned to be used again. Over and over, since the beginning of time, the same eternal energy has ebbed and flowed, fueling the efforts of mankind.

This is the reason each of us, from time to time, feels that at least some part of us may be eternal. In a very real sense, a part of us probably is eternal. Many people feel they have lived before; essentially, they have. And in essence, they will live again.

When creative energy is in heaven, it is called the Father. When it is in us, it is called the Son. When it returns to the source, it is the Holy Ghost.

Again and again, the same creative energy is breathed out, sent forth, and then breathed in again. We are all sons, daughters, and co-creators of heaven. Each of us keeps alive with a small piece of the whole, sent forth to fulfill heaven's dreams.

This is what I believe now, but my thinking about this subject will never end. I have promised myself to keep my mind and heart open to all ideas, past, present, and future. There is a Zen saying that in the beginner's eye, there are many possibilities. In an expert's eye, there are few. Or to quote Brancusi, "He who ceases to think like a child is already dead."

In November I went to a healing service at King's Chapel. It was for people in pain. Much to my surprise, there was a part of the service that included a laying on of hands for people who felt they needed it. Much to my surprise, I went forward, rationalizing that, if other animals besides man surround themselves by their kind in times of trouble, it was okay for me to do the same. As the minister put his hands on my head, two other people from the congregation closed in around me, and I let them absorb my hurt.

Now, as we are approaching Christmas, and it is a time for sharing, I will tell you this: I am not quite sure what we are supposed to discover here on earth, but I am quite convinced that we are supposed to discover it together.

This story is dedicated to my brother, Robert Christian Silchenstedt, who died of AIDS on August 30, 1988.

"The love never dies, Bertie."

When Lise finished reading, she passed a picture of her brother around the class. Each person held the picture for a moment or so in respect and reflection and then passed it on. There was total silence. It was one of those occasions when comments and criticism of any kind would have seemed like blasphemy.

These many months later I can only think of a single word I want to add, the word that comes to mind with the completion of every person's spiritual autobiography, the word with which it seems appropriate to end this book, in praise and gratitude for such people, such expression of the human spirit:

Amen.

# *Appendix*

*Suggested Plan for an Eight-Week Course*

*(meeting one evening a week)*

## SESSION 1

Welcome, definitions, guidelines, introductions.

Participants draw their favorite room in the house they grew up in.

Participants pair up and explain their rooms to each other.

Leader assigns two-page paper on childhood spiritual experience.

## SESSION 2

Participants read papers on childhood experience to group.

Participants draw the way they saw themselves and/or the way they saw God as a teenager.

Participants pair up and share pictures with each other.

Leader assigns two-page paper on adolescent spiritual experience.

Leader distributes teenage questionnaire; participants complete it in class and discuss, or take it home and write out answers.

Leader assigns dates for each person's reading of their eight-to-ten-page spiritual autobiography.

## SESSION 3

Participants read papers on adolescent spiritual experience to group.

Participants draw a friend, mentor, or "guide" who helped them on their spiritual journey.

Participants pair up and "introduce" the person they drew to each other.

Leader assigns two-page paper on friend, mentor or guide.

## SESSION 4

Participants read papers about friend, mentor, or guide.

Participants draw the "road map" of their spiritual journey.

Participants pair up and share the story of their journey.

Participants' take home the road maps to use them for reference or inspiration in writing their full autobiography. They may wish to keep it to use for further ideas, stories, or evocation of memories, if they continue to write after the end of the course.

## SESSIONS 5–8

Each of these evenings is devoted to reading the full autobiographies. No more than four people should read during one evening session.

## POTLUCK BANQUET FINALE

If possible, get together when the course is completed for a potluck supper in which everyone contributes something. Time can be spent enjoying the company of these people who have come to know and trust one another so deeply. This should be a fun and celebratory occasion.

*Suggested Schedule for a Weekend Retreat on Spiritual Autobiography*

FRIDAY EVENING

5:00–7:00 Arrival
7:00–8:00 Supper
8:00–9:30 Session 1
Leader sets out guidelines and definitions of course.
Participants draw a picture of "the present" and take a few
  minutes to explain their picture, as a way of introduction.
Prayer or meditation.
Observe silence for the rest of the evening.

SATURDAY

7:00–8:00 Breakfast
8:00–8:30 Morning service or meditation
9:00–12:00 Session 2
Participants draw their favorite room in the house they grew
  up in.
Participants pair up and explain their rooms to each other.
Leader reads a few short excerpts or papers about childhood
  spiritual experience to the group.
Participants take no more than forty-five minutes to think and
  write about a childhood spiritual experience.
Participants read aloud the paper just written.
12:00–1:00 Lunch
1:00–2:00 Free time for reading, walking, talking.
2:00–5:00 Session 3
Participants draw a friend, mentor, or guide who helped them
  on their spiritual journey.
Participants pair up and "introduce" the person they drew to
  each other.
Leader reads a few short excerpts about a friend, mentor, or
  guide.
Participants take no more than thirty minutes to write about
  how the friend, mentor, or guide helped them on their
  journey.
Participants read to the group the paper just written.

5:00–6:00 Free time

6:00–7:00 Evening service or meditation, perhaps with music.

7:00–8:00 Supper

8:00–10:00 Free time for some relaxing activity, games, music, singing, or other light entertainment.


**SUNDAY**


7:00–8:00 Breakfast

8:00–9:00 Morning service or meditation

9:00–12:00 Session 4

Participants read any papers written in previous sessions that time did not permit them to read earlier.

Participants take at least forty minutes to draw the road map of their spiritual journey, from birth to the present.

Participants pair up and each person takes twenty minutes to tell their partner about their map, and answer questions the partner may have.

Participants write an opening paragraph to their spiritual autobiography. If there is time, they may make notes or an outline for such a work.

Participants read to the group the opening of their spiritual autobiography.

12:00–1:00 Lunch

Conclusion

# A Brief Reading List
# in Spiritual Autobiography

Cowan, Paul. *An Orphan in History*. New York: Bantam, 1986. A journalist's story of his return to Judaism and discovery of his faith along with his roots.

Emerson, Ralph Waldo. *Essays of Ralph Waldo Emerson*. Cambridge, Mass.: Harvard University Press, 1987. The nineteenth-century transcendentalist's essays, especially "Self-Reliance," "The Over-Soul," and "The Address to the Harvard Divinity School" look at human life and the universe with connections to a higher spirit or power.

Griffin, Emilie. *Turning: Reflections on the Experience of Conversion*. New York: Harper and Row, 1984. A New York advertising woman tells the conversion stories of Merton and other Christian spiritual thinkers.

Kushner, Rabbi Harold. *When Bad Things Happen to Good People*. New York: Schocken Books, 1981. This widely read book is a spiritual guide for people struck by personal or family tragedies. It also describes the hard-won development of Rabbi Kushner's own faith through a searing experience of suffering and loss.

Lewis, C. S. *Surprised by Joy: The Shape of My Early Life*. New York: Harcourt Brace Jovanovich, 1956. The English author's discovery of faith that led to his career as a writer on Christianity.

Matthiessen, Peter. *Nine-Headed Dragon River: Zen Journals 1969–1982*. Boston: Shambhala Press, 1987. The Zen journals of this novelist's path to Buddhist monkhood.

Merton, Thomas. *Seven Storey Mountain*. New York: Harcourt Brace Jovanovich, 1948. A modern story of conversion, by a New York intellectual who became a Trappist monk.

Nelson, Shirley. *The Last Year of the War*. New York: Harper and Row, 1979. This autobiographical novel of a young woman's spiritual growth in a seminary during World War II takes an honest and eloquent look at the joys and difficulties of such a path.

———. *Fair, Clear, and Terrible: The Story of Shiloh, a Strange Fragment of American History*. Latham, N.Y.: British American Publishing, 1989. This historical account of a Christian sect that goes awry in a small town in Maine at the turn of the century is an exploration of the author's own family past. It is also a sober warning of the dangers of a too-naive and innocent faith which can lead even the most sincere believers to commit tragic acts in the name of God.

Tworkov, Helen. *Zen in America: Portraits of Five Teachers*. Berkeley, Calif.: North Point Press, 1989. An American student of Zen Buddhism perceptively illuminates the relevance of this practice to contemporary life in the United States.

Wiesel, Elie. *The Night Trilogy: Night, Dawn, The Accident*. New York: Hill and Wang, 1987. No serious investigation of spirituality in our time is complete without a knowledge of these works by this survivor of the Holocaust and winner of the Nobel Prize.